# The People of Calton Hill

The inscription to William Playfair's plan of 1819,
signed by the Lord Provost and others.

# The People of Calton Hill

## Ann Mitchell

JAMES THIN
THE MERCAT PRESS

First Published in 1993 by Mercat Press
James Thin, 53 South Bridge, Edinburgh EH1 1YS

ISBN 1873644 183

Set in Ehrhardt 11/13 point from author-generated discs by
Hewer Text Composition Services
Printed in Great Britain by The Cromwell Press, Melksham

# CONTENTS

# ILLUSTRATIONS

# ACKNOWLEDGEMENTS

Many people have contributed directly or indirectly to the collection of material for this book. I should particularly like to thank those who generously responded to a request for information by providing biographical details, family trees, photographs or other documents: Paul B Shaw, about his wife's great-great-grandfather; Robert Bartholomew, Donald Crabbie, Sue Matheson and John Warrack, about their great-grandfathers; Jack Nicholson about his grandfather and Agnes Poole who wrote about her aunt and uncle.

My warm thanks also go to others who kindly talked to me about their lives in the area in the first two decades of this century: Albert Barnet, Alison Barr, Betsy Hume (née Simpson), and Ailsa Inglis; to those who told me about living here in the next two decades: James Bertram, Rosemary Brown Douglas, Isla Burnet (née Anderson), Marion Green, David Hyslop, Janet Tait (née Morrison) and Gordon Thornton, and to Joe Kidd and Sir William Murrie who lived here more recently and provided anecdotes and references.

I am also grateful to Janet Adam Smith and Archie Turnbull who gave useful contacts; to the staff of the Edinburgh Room, Central Library for their unfailing patience and helpfulness; to present neighbours in the area and to my husband Angus for his constant encouragement.

# BIOGRAPHICAL NOTE

Ann Mitchell was born and educated in Oxford where she obtained a degree in mathematics. She spent the last two years of the war at Bletchley Park, working on the German Enigma codes. After many years in counselling and administration with the Marriage Guidance Council, she undertook sociological research at the University of Edinburgh. Her investigation into childrens' experiences of divorce (*Children in the Middle*) led her to write books for separating couples and their children.

Ann and her husband Angus have lived for forty years in Regent Terrace, where they brought up their four children. She was therefore ideally placed to research the lives of past residents of the area in which she has lived for so long.

# INTRODUCTION

People breathe life into houses and this book is an account of some of the people who lived in the eastern extension of the New Town of Edinburgh, on the slopes of Calton Hill. Others have written of the architecture and the history of the area, but little is known about the people.

Edinburgh Town Council held an architectural competition in 1812 for the development of housing to the east of Craig's successful New Town. None of the thirty-two entries was accepted because they all included a formal lay-out of streets on the hill. However the report of the architect William Stark fired the imagination with his insistence on the importance of following the natural contours of the hillside on a site which was quite unlike that of the New Town.

Stark himself died but the planned construction of Waterloo Place in 1818-22 led to his pupil William Playfair being commissioned to produce a plan for a 'proposed New Town between Edinburgh and Leith'. His 1819 plan included an elaborate lay-out of streets to the north of London Road, of which only a small portion was built. More importantly, he designed a scheme to build prestigious houses on the eastern slope of Calton Hill, to which he hoped to attract a 'circle of fashionable and wealthy people'.

Playfair's scheme was accepted although there was, as yet, no access road to the site from Princes Street.

A joint committee from the feu superiors of this area - George Heriot's Hospital, Trinity Hospital and Mr Alexander Allan of Hillside (a banker) - agreed to make available the land required; the feus were advertised and building started. Meanwhile public buildings appearing on Calton Hill drew the eye from Princes Street to this whole area, and their history is briefly described here. Mr Allan died in 1825 and never saw the completed Terraces. He and his wife and eleven children are commemorated in Old Calton Burying Ground, together with Bell Begbie 'the faithful and affectionate nurse' to all his children and 'an esteemed servant in his family for 57 years' who died at the age of ninety-one.

Playfair's 'circle of fashionable and wealthy people' did not materialise in

Playfair's plan, the northern part of which was never implemented.

the way he had expected. Many citizens who fitted that description had already made their homes in Craig's New Town. Early residents tended to be people of independent means, solicitors or retired Army officers of the East India Company: wine and tea merchants soon followed. They mostly came from the fringes of the New Town or from outside Edinburgh; a few came from George Square.

The streets were named for historical reasons. Waterloo Place was named after the Duke of Wellington's victory over Napoleon in 1815. Royal and Regent Terraces derived from the visit to Edinburgh in 1822 of George IV, lately Regent during the incapacity of his father, George III. Carlton Place (which later became Carlton Terrace) referred to Carlton House, the king's London home when he had been Prince Regent.

A directory has been compiled by the writer of some 800 householders who have lived in Regent, Royal and Carlton Terraces up to the Second World War. This was done by reference to the Post Office street directories, which listed individuals in alphabetical order for the whole of Edinburgh before 1832 and within streets after that date, and are fairly comprehensive up to 1940. This directory has been deposited in the Edinburgh Room of the Edinburgh Central Library, where it can be consulted.

An examination of this directory shows quite a number of householders who moved from one house to another and also several families which spread into two or more houses, as sons or brothers acquired homes near to the houses in which they had grown up.

From these 800 names, a selection has been made for this book of some of the more interesting past residents, of whom some were well-known and some not. Inevitably some have been excluded who would have been equally interesting. Families who lived in Waterloo Place and Calton Hill have been included. Children, grandchildren and great-grandchildren have generously provided useful information about their families who lived in the area.

The residents described were not necessarily the owners of the houses they lived in. Many houses were rented in the nineteenth century. For instance, my own house, 20 Regent Terrace, belonged to successive members of one family, that of Sir Robert Preston, Baronet, of Valleyfield and Lutton, for seventy-five years but none of them ever lived in it.

Apart from the residents, there are records of well-known visitors to houses in the three terraces. These include the heir to the French throne, Thomas Carlyle, John Stuart Mill, Henry Stanley, G K Chesterton, Hilaire Belloc, Queen Mary, Pablo Casals, General de Gaulle and Kathleen Ferrier.

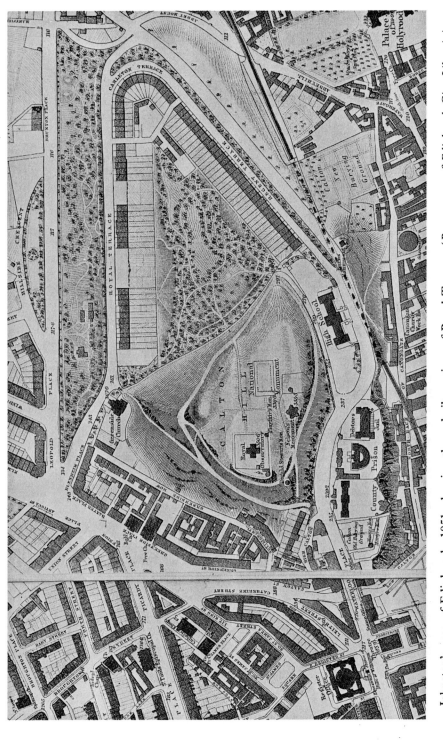

Johnston's map of Edinburgh, 1851, showing the unbuilt sections of Royal Terrace. (*By courtesy of Edinburgh City Libraries*).

# 1.
# CALTON HILL

Looking eastwards along Princes Street, the view is dominated by Calton Hill, only half a mile away and with some striking buildings on the skyline. The hill was once part of the Barony of Calton.

The land has a long history. James II of Scotland granted the north west slope of the hill to the citizens of Edinburgh in 1456 for tilts and tournaments. A Carmelite monastery was founded there in 1518. In 1534 two martyrs of the reformation, Norman Gourlay and David Stratoun were burned to death on the northern slope, so that the inhabitants of Fife, seeing the fire, 'might be stricken with terroure and feare'. Shortly after that, a lepers' hospital was built there. The inmates were forbidden to leave the site on pain of hanging, and a gibbet was erected at one end of the hospital.

Edinburgh Town Council purchased the lands of Calton from Lord Balmerino in 1724, but there was some confusion thereafter as to the powers and privileges of members of the Incorporated Trades of Calton. It was not clear who was responsible for the maintenance of the area, and who was allowed to trade. The collection of manure from the streets covered the expense of lighting the streets by oil lamps.

The Barony of Calton in 1833 included the hill itself and all the buildings along its base to the south, west and north sides. The eastern boundary was the wall of the new private gardens of Regent, Royal and Carlton Terraces. The houses on the west side, built in the 1760s, formed a street called Calton Hill, whose inhabitants will be described shortly. The Barony was formally abolished by an Act of 1856.

## Preachers

The slopes of Calton Hill provided space in the eighteenth century for large open-air congregations to hear popular preachers.

John Wesley, a fiery and impetuous Methodist, travelled around Britain preaching for sixty years. In May 1764 he preached on Calton Hill to a huge crowd for one and a half hours on a Saturday during the church's General Assembly. He recorded in his journal that many ministers were there but 'the wind was high and sharp and blew away a few delicate ones; but most of the congregation did not stir till I had concluded'. He preached on other days, apparently to crowds of five or six thousand, even at five o'clock in the morning or at nine in the evening, continuing up to midnight.

In 1798 the celebrated preacher the Rev. Rowland Hill (son of Sir Rowland Hill, baronet, of Shropshire) visited Edinburgh for the first time. He preached in some churches but the crowds became so vast that he was persuaded to hold forth from a platform erected on the Calton Hill (at the place where the jail later stood), where his audience was reckoned as not less than 10,000. He preached there several times more and on the last occasion, when a collection was made for the charity workhouse, it was said that 20,000 people were present.

## The Jews' Grave

A German-born Jew called Heyman Lyon, who was a dentist and corn operator at Reid's Court in the Canongate, asked the Town Council in 1795 for burial ground for himself and his Dutch wife Hana. He did not want to lie in a Christian burying-ground, and was granted a site in the rock on the north side of the recently erected Observatory. The site was closed by a gate. It disappeared many years later, when the footpath round the observatory was widened.

## The Washing Green

Lord Cockburn, in an open letter to the Lord Provost in 1849 (*On the best ways of spoiling the beauties of Edinburgh*) protested, among other things, against the proposal to set aside part of the higher ground of Calton Hill for a public washing green with water laid on, which would lead to worn turf and mud, fires, poles and ropes. He acknowledged that the whole hill had always been a public drying green.

Perhaps his protests were in vain, for Lord Kingsburgh (Lord Justice Clerk) said of Calton Hill that the upper part was frequently used as a place for beating carpets, which sent clouds of insanitary dust over the neighbouring ground. 'On the north slope, linen was washed and the ground slopped around water-cocks which should never have been allowed to disfigure the scene'.

NINTY FOUR YEARS HAVE I 226
SOJOURNED UPON THIS EARTH
ENDEAVOURING TO DO GOOD

The Rev. John Wesley returning from preaching on Calton Hill in 1837,
accompanied by two ministers. (*Kay's Portraits*).

## Observatories

The summit of Calton Hill was an ideal place for an observatory, proposed by Thomas Short, optician, to house telescopes manufactured by his internationally known brother James in London. An observatory was designed by James Craig and building began in 1776. Thomas Short set up home in its Gothic tower but the building progressed very slowly and he died before it was completed in 1792.

The finished building was a poor substitute for the original design and was deemed unsuitable for its purpose. It was replaced by William Playfair's New Observatory in 1818. This building was in cruciform shape with a central dome, and in 1822 became the Royal Observatory although not yet equipped with instruments or telescopes. Peter McArthur, an assistant at the Observatory, lived in Thomas Short's former house in the Old Observatory.

Thomas Henderson was appointed Royal Astronomer and Professor of Practical Astronomy in 1834. His assistant observer Alexander Wallace lived in the Old Observatory House, at first sharing it with a burying ground watchman and his wife and son. Wallace never married and by 1861 lived there alone with one female servant. He was chief observer at the Observatory until 1880.

Meanwhile, in 1827 Miss Maria Theresa Short, Thomas's daughter, laid claim to her father's instruments. She then built a small wooden observatory within the fence which enclosed the National Monument, to which she charged the public for admission. This practice continued until 1850 when, after complaints about the inferiority of her so-called scientific exhibits and the unsavoury characters who were attracted there, she was evicted and her observatory demolished. She took her Camera Obscura to a site on Castlehill, where it remains to this day, in the Outlook Tower.

After Henderson's death at the age of forty-six, Charles Piazzi Smyth became Astronomer Royal for Scotland from 1846 to 1888. He had inadequate financial support from the government and had to pay out of his own pocket for the repair and replacement of instruments. Members of a Government Commission of Inquiry were strongly critical in 1876 of the state of the instruments of the Observatory. A Royal Commission on Scottish Universities proposed the abolition of the Royal Observatory and the separation of the posts of Regius Professor of Astronomy and Astronomer Royal for Scotland. Eventually a new Royal Observatory was built on Blackford Hill in 1896, while the old one became the City Observatory which was closed in 1937.

The official residence of Piazzi Smyth and his successor Ralph Copeland was at 15 Royal Terrace and their careers are further described in Chapter 4.

The Old Observatory House continued to be occupied as a keeper's house. In 1881 the tenant was an observatory attendant and his wife with, strangely as a sub-tenant, the chief assistant astronomer Thomas Heath who was unmarried.

## Playfair Memorial

Set in the surrounding wall of the Observatory is a square Greek-style monument to Professor John Playfair, uncle of the architect William Playfair. John Playfair, as Professor of Mathematics, had been closely involved in setting up the original observatory. Lord Cockburn said he was 'admired by all men and beloved by all women; no one who knew him can ever resist basking in his remembrance.'

## Nelson Monument

Shortly after the victorious Battle of Trafalgar in 1805, the people of Edinburgh decided to mark the death of Admiral Lord Nelson in the battle by the erection of a monument on Calton Hill. The first design, by Alexander Nasmyth, was rejected as being too expensive. An alternative design by Robert Burn for a monument in the shape of Nelson's famous telescope was accepted.

The foundation stone was laid in 1807. Those responsible had decided against a public ceremony partly because of 'the loss and expense which would thus have been occasioned to individuals, and the idleness and debauchery to which such events always give rise' and partly because of the risk of an accident if a large crowd were to assemble on the precipitous site. Indeed, Grant, in *Old and New Edinburgh*, reported that in 1828 'a mass of rock, fully fifty tons in weight, fell from under Nelson's monument and crashed to the roadway below'.

The monument, which was more than 100 feet high, was not completed until 1815, when Thomas Bonnar added the accommodation at the base, although the principal tower had been nearly finished in 1808.

Over the doorway Nelson's crest can still be seen and also a model of the stern of the *San Josef*, the Spanish admiral's flagship at the Battle of Cape St.Vincent in 1797. Nelson captured the ship, and the Spanish admiral was killed. To either side of the door were two stained glass windows, showing Nelson himself and various trophies. These windows have long since disappeared.

The rooms at the base, originally intended for accommodation for a naval officer and a few disabled seamen, were instead leased to the widow of a petty officer. She was allowed to sell confectionery, soup and other light food, but not wine or strong drink. The restaurant was sometimes used for

Old Observatory House, Dugald Stewart's Monument, the Playfair Memorial, the National Monument and the Nelson Monument, with Old Calton Burying Ground on both sides of Waterloo Place, c.1900.

private occasions. For instance, in 1826 some twenty gentlemen of the Ayr and Edinburgh Burns Club held their eighth annual celebration there. The Lord Provost wanted to close this facility on Sundays in 1849 in case of unseemly behaviour. It had been the custom for thirty-five years for families to go on Sunday evenings to partake of biscuits, lemonade and ginger beer. It was pointed out to the Lord Provost that temperance public houses and coffee rooms were also open on Sundays. There has always been a resident custodian.

In 1852 Professor Piazzi Smyth arranged for the time-signal of a ball on the top of the Nelson Monument to be raised to a cross-bar shortly before 1 pm and dropped at 1 pm. This was for the benefit of ships in the Forth, who no longer had to send someone to town to set their chronometers. He improved this service to the public in 1861, when he started the custom of firing the one o'clock gun from Edinburgh Castle, which was controlled from the Observatory. James Ritchie, clockmakers of Leith Street, erected a steel wire directly connecting the Castle with the Nelson Monument, a distance of 4,020 feet. Both time-signals are still in operation daily, and an employee of James Ritchie still winds up the time-ball manually.

The Old and New Observatories.

## *Flags Flying*

The top of the monument provides a splendid place from which to fly a flag. This was first done in 1810, on the occasion of the great public funeral of Lord Provost William Coulter, when a flag was hoisted at half mast and two streamers of black crepe were displayed from the top. In 1842 a red flag was to have been flown on the monument to signal Queen Victoria's arrival at Granton in the royal yacht, after which two guns were to be fired from the Castle. Unfortunately, there was no flag available and the citizens waited in vain to hear the guns fired.

For some years a flag was hoisted on the monument whenever a consignment of the latest London fashions arrived at Leith harbour: Edinburgh ladies could then hasten to Princes Street shops to make their purchases.

The date of Nelson's victory at the Battle of Trafalgar was marked for at

Nelson's signal on Trafalgar Day.

least part of the eighteenth century by the raising of a standard on the monument. Since before the beginning of this century, on 21 October, which is the anniversary of the battle, Nelson's naval signal has been flown: 'England expects this day that every man will do his duty'.

More recently, and certainly in the 1960s and 1970s, a flag was flown from the monument if a royal garden party at Holyrood Palace had to be cancelled because of bad weather. Guests could note that signal instead of setting out for the palace in the rain.

## National Monument

The next large building on Calton Hill was to be the National Monument. In 1819 a group of noblemen and gentlemen, under the chairmanship of the Duke of Atholl, agreed to construct a replica of the Parthenon to commemorate men who had fallen in the Napoleonic Wars. An earlier design, by Archibald Elliot, had shown 'a great pillared portico leading to a great domed Inscription Hall and, beyond that, to a church'. The proposed site was at the south end of the Mound. However, that plan was discarded and William Playfair's design was accepted. His building, also, was to incorporate a church.

A public appeal was launched and the foundation stone, weighing six tons, was laid in 1822 by the Duke of Hamilton, although only £16,000 had been promised towards the target of £42,000. Playfair reported in 1825 that it took twelve horses and seventy men to move some of the larger stones up the hill.

The next year George Cleghorn of Weens, WS, who later lived at 24 Regent Terrace, was scathing about advertisements for proposed burial vaults under the monument. He recommended spending the money, instead, on an equestrian statue of George IV in front of the building.

By 1829 the project had to be abandoned owing to lack of funds, and the resulting 'ruin' of twelve pillars remains as a prominent part of Edinburgh's skyline. Playfair described it as 'a striking proof of the pride and poverty of us Scots'.

Over the years a number of unsuccessful proposals have been made for the completion of the monument. For instance, in 1906 a Mr William Mitchell, SSC, launched an appeal for the National Monument to be completed and to house a Scottish National Gallery of modern art, with a funicular railway from Waterloo Place.

## Statuary

Robert Forrest, a Lanarkshire stonemason, built a hall in 1832 behind the National Monument to house an exhibition of thirty groups of his own statuary, under the auspices of the Royal Association of Contributors to the National Monument. He used huge blocks of stone from Craigleith quarry, each weighing over five tons. From these he made historical and other statues including such figures as Robert the Bruce, the Duke of Wellington, Robert Burns and an equestrian statue of the conversion of St Paul. He and his wife had their home in Calton Hill Cottage, which has long since disappeared. His widow was still there at the 1861 census, described as 'exhibitor of statuary'. The exhibits were sold at auction in 1876 as being desirable decorations for gentlemen's policies.

Robert Forrest prepared three alternative plans for a memorial to the Duke of Wellington which the Earl of Elgin proposed, in 1838, should be on the summit of Arthur's Seat. Lord Elgin chose the 80 foot high plan, which was not equestrian, but he died before his proposal could be implemented.

By 1881 the Forrests' house had become the home of the keeper of the National Monument and his wife and three children - the fourteen year old daughter being a dressmaker.

## Dugald Stewart's Monument

Playfair designed yet another Greek-style monument on Calton Hill. This circular one built in 1832, was to Dugald Stewart who died in 1828. He had been, first Professor of Mathematics jointly with his father and then of Moral Philosophy. Lord Cockburn had attended his lectures which he found 'like the opening of the heavens. I felt that I had a soul'.

## The Calton Hill Cannon

Another landmark on the hill, and popular with children, is the old brass cannon which is trained on Princes Street. It had a chequered history, being made in Portugal in the seventeenth century, and then being sent to the Portuguese East Indies. It next became the property of the King of Arakan, on the west coast of Burma, from where it was captured in 1785 by the Burmese, and an inscription in Burmese records this event. It fell into British hands in 1885 after the capture of Mandalay and was presented to the City of Edinburgh and placed on Calton Hill. Five other old guns on Calton Hill were removed in 1940 in the war-time drive for scrap metal for the manufacture of armaments.

## Valhalla

In 1909 Henry F Kerr, ARIBA, produced a plan for an open-air Valhalla or a Park of Memories on Calton Hill. He proposed a large bandstand to the north of the National Monument, a theatre of 4,500 seats for pageants, plays, music or speeches, two fountains and several of the footpaths to become carriage roads with a dozen view-points. Nothing came of this plan.

## Old Observatory House

This house, which had been the home of observatory staff, continued to be occupied by tenants. In 1963 it was advertised to let and prospective tenants were invited to suggest a rent. The house then had two public rooms and a kitchen on the ground floor and three bedrooms and a bathroom on the upper floor. The basement still contained the old kitchen and wash-house. A retired naval commander and his wife lived there for nearly thirty years, but the house is now uninhabited.

## Full Circle

An ancient Celtic May Day festival of Beltane used to take place on Calton Hill. Cattle, crops and humans were blessed, fires were lit, plays and sporting events took place. Since 1988 the annual Beltane Fire has been revived, attended by many people as well as by electronically amplified music until the early hours of the morning.

## Alternative Verdicts on the Hill

Charles Dickens described Calton Hill as 'littered over with waste fancies – a rubbish heap of the imaginative architecture – a hill to be looked from with an elevation of the spirit but to be looked at with an elevation of the nose'.

In contrast, Prof.A J Youngson wrote in 1966 that, while the hill was indeed littered with buildings, mostly classical, they made a 'seemingly fanciful arrangement of harmonious composition which forms a pattern constantly and wonderfully changing as one looks up or across at the hill'.

# CALTON HILL – THE STREET

Somewhat confusingly, the steep hill which winds its way up the western edge of Calton Hill, from Leith Street to Waterloo Place, is itself called Calton Hill. It was the only route to the (Old) Calton Burying Ground until Regent Bridge was built in 1819.

Houses in this street were the earliest to be built in the area and were virtually an extension of the Old Town, although the New Town was beginning. They were built on both sides of the street, starting from the bottom, in the 1760s. The first four feuars were a wright, a mason, a cooper

Aerial view of Regent (to the left), Royal (to the right) and Carlton Terraces and the Mews, with Princes Street and the St James Centre at the top. (*Sarah Noble*)

and a bricklayer. The cooper was Andrew Syme, who feued the lowest stance on the north side and after whom, presumably, Syme's Court was named. This court (which no longer exists) had six small houses in it in 1807. By 1861 there were twenty households in Sim's (or Syme's) Court which were all part of 8 Calton Hill. They must indeed have been small. As the houses progressed up the hill they became more substantial. The last house on the north side was no. 28, later called Rock House, home for nearly thirty years of William Menzies, WS, from 1765. He was first a procurator and then a solicitor in the custom house.

Among other early residents were Walter Hogg, accountant and assistant manager of the British Linen company in Abbeyhill, Thomas Ogilvie, writer (ie solicitor) and James Gordon, another accountant. Gordon's address was Horn's Building, Calton Hill, where another resident in the 1780s was Donald McNab, writer. Non-resident owners included Sir Alexander Dick, baronet, of Prestonfield, a physician, and Christopher Irvine late of the Island of Tobago but by now residing in London.

## Link with Robert Burns

The best known early resident was Mrs Agnes Maclehose, better remembered as Robert Burns' Clarinda. According to the Post Office Directory, she came to live at 14 Calton Hill in 1800. She was a great beauty who had married at the age of seventeen a Glasgow lawyer, after a courtship begun on a stage-coach between Edinburgh and Glasgow.

It was an unhappy marriage and Mrs Maclehose soon left her husband, coming to live in Potter Row in Edinburgh in 1782. She was financially supported partly by an annuity left by her father and partly by her cousin, who later became a Scottish judge, Lord Craig. In Edinburgh she filled her leisure hours by cultivating her literary tastes and she met Robert Burns at a friend's house in 1787.

Shortly afterwards Burns became housebound, having injured his knee in a fall from a coach, so he could not visit Mrs Maclehose. They frequently corresponded and she used to send him verses she had written, some of which he had published in the *Musical Museum*. She sent him the verse 'When first you saw Clarinda's charms' and they thereafter called each other Clarinda and Sylvander.

For two years they enjoyed a close (but probably platonic) friendship, mainly through their letters, after which Burns married Jean Armour. They subsequently met only once more but their correspondence continued until 1792, by which time Mrs Maclehose had returned from a brief but unsuccessful reconciliation with her husband in Jamaica. Burns died in 1796, but his Clarinda lived at 14 Calton Hill until her death in 1841.

## Boys who Made Good

By that time, two boys who were to become famous had been born at 5 Calton Hill. They were Daniel and George Wilson, two of the eleven children of a wine merchant at Regent Arch. Most of the children died in childhood. Born in 1816 and 1818 Daniel and George attended the Royal High School before and after the new school was built in Regent Road.

The two boys watched the boring of the railway tunnel through part of Calton Hill. When it was opened, Daniel reported

> a good, honest quadruped, fed on oats and hay and not on coal or coke, drew the rude railway carriage at an exceedingly safe and moderate pace. Sometimes a Musselburgh fishwife would hail the driver, who would stop the train till the creel and its owner got leisurely on board.

Sir Daniel Wilson, as he became, was an antiquarian and historian. He began his career in London, writing for the literary press, but soon returned to Edinburgh, publishing *Memorials of Edinburgh in Olden Times*, and then his great work *The Archaeology and Prehistoric Annals of Scotland*. He left his native country in 1853 to become Professor of History and English Literature at Toronto University, refusing the offer of the principalship of McGill University, Montreal. He crowned his career by becoming President of Toronto University. He had successfully campaigned for a system of national education, instead of sectarian or denominational colleges.

The younger brother, George, precociously founded a 'juvenile society for the advancement of knowledge' before going to the High School at the age of ten. He later qualified as a surgeon but disliked medicine and switched to chemistry and lectured on that subject in Edinburgh University to medical students.

Dr George Wilson, FRSE, became an expert on colour-blindness and realised the importance of testing railway personnel and sailors for that defect. He became Director of the Scottish Industrial Museum and Regius Professor of Technology in Edinburgh. He became an early enthusiast for the use of anaesthesia, sometimes looked on as a luxury. At the age of twenty-five he had his left foot amputated and afterwards wrote to Sir James Young Simpson of 'the black whirlwind of emotion, the horror of great darkness, and the sense of desertion by God and man' that swept through him during the operation. He was buried in Old Calton Burying Ground.

## Early Householders

In 1833 the Post Office street directory listed thirty-six separate households in this street, mostly of artisans. At the time of the 1841 census there were over sixty households: this increase was probably because the census, unlike the Post Office, listed lodgers as separate householders. There were some fresh occupations such as paper stainer, carver and gilder, missionary and quill dresser. With 324 residents, the street must have been teeming with people. Perhaps that was why Lord Cockburn described it as 'the steep, narrow, stinking, spiral street'.

Several families had five or six small children and a few had a resident servant, an architect having two. The youngest resident servant was a girl aged ten. There were at least three lodging houses. Other householders were five shoemakers, two letter-carriers, two spirit-dealers and two clothiers. The remaining occupations included a bit and spur maker, who lived in number 1 for over thirty years, a mail-guard and a coach-guard, a saddle-tree maker and a music seller. Many of them had their businesses round the corner, in Low Calton or Calton Road.

## *Distinguished Photographers*

Rock House, one of the few houses in Edinburgh with a fine view to the north and the south, was then occupied by Ninian Stevenson, a writing master with a middle-aged woman servant. Two years later Robert Adamson came to live in Edinburgh at Rock House where he established a photographic studio in which he was soon joined by David Octavius Hill. Adamson died in 1848 and Hill made this his home until his death in 1870.

A landscape painter and book illustrator, Hill had over 270 paintings exhibited at the Royal Scottish Academy, where he became the first Secretary, a post he held for most of his life. He needed the studio in his house for his pioneering use of calotype photographs, especially as aids for his massive painting of the 450 Disruption ministers signing the Act of Separation and Deed of Demission in 1843. He spent twenty-three years working on this painting which can now be seen in the Free Church Assembly Hall. Hill's second wife was Amelia Paton, herself a portrait painter. She was also one of the many sculptors responsible for the statues on the Scott Monument representing characters from his novels.

David Hill invited Thomas Annan, one of the most important nineteenth century photographers, to bring his family to Rock House in 1869. The Annans remained for six months, while Thomas shared the studio.

The next occupier of Rock House was Archibald Burns, who made a photographic record of Edinburgh during his ten years there from 1870.

Rock House continued to be home and studio to photographers. Three generations of one family covered sixty-five years there until 1945. First came Alexander Adam Inglis, then one of his sons Francis Caird Inglis (photographer to Edward VII and George V) and then his grandson of the same name, Alexander Adam.

Rock House photographed in 1874 by Alexander Burns, who had his studio there. (*By courtesy of Edinburgh City Libraries*).

## Increasing Population

The overcrowding worsened, for there were 417 people registered at the 1861 census, ninety-six of them described as heads of households. Twelve of these households shared one lodging-house at no. 7, one comprising a husband, wife, six children and a servant.

A number of residents were masters of their trades. A tobacco manufacturer employed four men and twelve boys, a bell-hanger six men and two boys, while a boot and shoe maker employed fourteen men. A master clockmaker, William Ott, born in Germany, was one of seven householders at no. 4. Some residents had apprentices living with them, while others took on neighbours' sons as apprentices. Surprisingly, only one warder from the prison over the road lived in the street in 1861.

Women had occupations such as dressmaker, straw hat maker, bookfolder or washerwoman. One widow was described as 'keeper mangle', so perhaps her neighbours paid her for the use of her mangle. Children had employment from the age of twelve: one was a bookseller's message boy, another a waiter in a spirit shop and a girl was a milliner's apprentice.

One family consisted of two sisters, the head of household being aged sixty-eight and unmarried and described as 'pauper – was never from home'. Her seventy-year-old sister was married but her husband was in Morningside Lunatic Asylum.

A thirty-year-old unmarried woman whose occupation was given as domestic servant was a visitor in one household where she gave birth to a boy on the night of the census.

The population density was only marginally less by 1881, with 381 people spread over eighty-four households, eighteen of which were in Sim's Court. Apart from mundane occupations such as bootmaker, tinsmith and flesher there were some more exotic ones. These included tobacco spinner, mosaic tile layer, marble mason and an unemployed bottle washer. No wives were in employment, but one 25-year-old woman visitor was a hawker, an occupation which until recently led to householders affixing a 'no hawkers' sign on their front doors or gates.

A few professional people had arrived in Calton Hill. An architect, James W Smith, made his lodging at no.7 in the home of a railway porter. A widowed assistant curator of the National Museum of Antiquities, George Hastie, was one of three householders at no. 26, with his ten-year-old daughter and a seed merchant and nurseryman as a lodger.

## Twentieth Century

During and after the First World War there was a great community spirit among the residents of Calton Hill, who held street parties with bonfires.

However there was a social divide and the children who lived in the top half of the street were not allowed to play with those in the lower half, where the houses had degenerated into slums. Number 10 housed a dance hall which was also forbidden territory.

Even the higher houses were fairly primitive. On the first floor Mr and Mrs James Simpson with their five children at no.24 took in lodgers, one of whom had an early gramophone with a horn in the early 1920s, and another had one of the first crystal radio sets with a cat's whisker. There was only one cold water tap to serve eleven people, but they did have a flush W C . One of the Simpson daughters lives there now as a widow.

Some houses still had no lavatories of their own, and two black doors still visible below no.20 led to outside lavatories for prison warders who lived in two or three houses half way down the hill, including no.13, the circular tower, which now lies empty.

At the foot of the hill stood Jessie with her barrow piled high with fruit for sale. Jessie had voluminous skirts and, lacking access to a lavatory, she used to straddle the gutter in full view of passers by. Round the corner from the bottom of the hill were cafes, a tobacco factory, a bakery and a variety of shops. One was a bookshop, with books displayed on the pavement. A book could be borrowed from Saturday till Tuesday midday for two old pence.

Another door, still to be seen in the wall at the top of the street, was where Harry the news-vendor parked his newspaper stand when it was not in use.

The hill was so steep that many accidents occurred, especially involving horses. A carter would have a wedge on a rope in the wide square gutter (still there today) to hold back the horses. But the horses were still apt to fall, and sparks flew as their hooves scrambled on the setts.

One of the gardens on Calton Hill contains a stone monument about eight feet high, depicting an eagle, a serpent, a lion and a bear. Its origin is unknown and symbolism obscure.

Demolition of the houses on the south side and of the lower half of the north side began in the 1930s. Gas Board offices appeared on the south side and a biscuit factory on the north. The remaining houses on the north side present a picturesque sight, some with pretty front gardens. Front doors are at many different levels and set back from the street in different ways. All are reached by a flight of steps, either up or down: none are at pavement level. Inside, some stairs are like a rabbit warren, because houses have been divided or combined. What was once a flat at no.26 was incorporated into Rock House, no.28, after the Second World War.

# 2.
# WATERLOO PLACE AND REGENT ROAD

Princes Street was originally blocked at its east end by a row of houses facing it. They backed on to what was to become Waterloo Place. The land to the east was already in use for the Calton Burying Ground and for the Bridewell, both of which were approached by the narrow, steep and winding street called Calton Hill.

A proposal to demolish these houses and to build a new road to the east involved bridging the fifty foot deep ravine of the Low Calton and cutting through the burying ground. Robert Stevenson, FRSE, (grandfather of RLS) was appointed the engineer and in 1815 the foundation stone of the bridge was laid with a procession of 2,000 masons from the High Church to the site, in spite of unfavourable weather. Stevenson was anxious to preserve the views to the Forth in the north and to the Old Town in the south and therefore stressed the importance of leaving open the sides of the proposed bridge with no buildings on it. For four years, Stevenson worked without payment, although he himself paid an assistant.

In 1816 Archibald Elliot was appointed architect. He did not take up the suggestion of the architect William Stark, that the bridge should be built like a Roman aquaduct with two or three rows of arcades, to be made into workshops, with stairs leading to the road below at either end of the bridge.

Regent Bridge was completed by 1819 and was officially opened for the visit to Edinburgh of Prince Leopold of Saxe-Coburg, Queen Victoria's favourite uncle and afterwards King of Belgium.

It was said that when King George IV's carriage drove round the bend of Regent Road on his state visit in 1822 he saw the massed crowds on Calton Hill and exclaimed, 'My God! that is altogether overpowering', and burst

The Theatre Royal in Shakespeare Square, on the site of the present Head Post Office, from a watercolour by John Le Conte. (*City Art Centre, Edinburgh*).

into tears. Keen to make his visit a success, he had spent over £1,000 on new clothes, including a kilt.

## *Theatre Royal*

At the western extremity of Waterloo Place on the south side, was the Theatre Royal in Shakespeare Square. The theatre was opened in 1769. It was elegantly fitted out inside, with seats in a pit, two galleries and boxes, but it was criticised for being plain outside. The principal features were a statue of Shakespeare on the highest point of the roof, over the main entrance, flanked by statues of the Muses of Tragedy and Comedy on two lower pinnacles.

The celebrated Mrs Sarah Siddons appeared there in 1784 and again in 1815, when she gave a benefit performance for her grandchildren. King George IV attended a performance at the Theatre Royal of *Rob Roy MacGregor* in 1822. Sir Walter Scott (on whose book the play was based) and Mr W H Murray, the manager, escorted the King to his special box, each carrying a silver candlestick. Four hours before the doors opened at 6 pm a huge crowd had gathered for the pit and gallery seats. Mrs Harriet Siddons (wife of Henry and daughter-in-law of Sarah and also sister of Mr Murray) was in the cast. Harriet and Henry Siddons lived successively in York Place, Picardy Place and Windsor Street.

*Rob Roy* was again presented to a royal audience in 1962 on the occasion of the state visit to Edinburgh of King Olav of Norway in the Lyceum Theatre. The Queen, the Duke of Edinburgh, the Queen Mother, Princess Margaret and other members of the royal family were present.

Sarah Sibbald, 'Apple Glory', outside the Theatre Royal.
(*Life Jottings of an Old Edinburgh Citizen*).

Shakespeare Square was partly demolished in 1815 to open up the space for Waterloo Place. The theatre and adjacent buildings were bought in 1854 with a view to erecting a new post office on the site, where the present Head Post Office stands. The theatre was demolished for that purpose in 1859. By that time there were a number of theatres in Edinburgh, although the Theatre Royal had been the only one at the start of the century.

Sarah Sibbald, with cheeks as rosy as her best apples, had a fruit barrow at the corner of the Theatre Royal. When the sheds were put up for the erection of the new Post Office, the Board of Works installed her on a raised dais in the corner where, sheltered from the weather, she carried on her business in great style.

## The Calton Burying Ground

The population of Edinburgh was increasing by the eighteenth century, and the residents of Calton were in the parish of South Leith, which was inconveniently far away for burials. A fresh burying ground was needed and the land to the south east of Calton Hill was chosen. The original area was to the north of what is now Waterloo Place.

The first burial was in 1719, of Jean Willocks, when the ground extended to half an acre. More ground was gradually added from 1724 and sheep were pastured there until 1760 to keep the ground in good condition. Meanwhile, 'Toms and children did greatlie abuse the grass'.

Many famous and interesting people were buried here. Robert Adam designed a large circular tower as a monument to David Hume the philosopher, who died in 1776. An obelisk was erected in 1844 to the memory of Thomas Muir and the four other political martyrs who argued for parliamentary reform, were charged with sedition and were transported in 1793 to Botany Bay for fourteen years. Only one of them returned alive. Lord Cockburn described the monument as 'a pillar of disgrace to the delinquent judges'.

A mausoleum commemorating Robert Burn, designer of the Nelson Monument, was erected in 1816 by his wife and twelve surviving children. A memorial to the Scottish soldiers who fell in the American Civil War shows life-size figures of President Abraham Lincoln emancipating a slave, both being in bronze.

An interesting inscription on the Rev. James Millar's stone records that he founded a bursary for a student of divinity 'which student is to pay the feu duty of this burial-ground, being one penny per year, to keep the stone in good repair'. Mr Millar, who died in 1801, was chaplain to several city charities.

Archibald Campbell Tait, a former pupil of the Royal High School, later headmaster of Rugby School and Archbishop of Canterbury erected a stone to the memory of Betty Morton, faithful nurse to the family of his father, Crawford Tait Esq, who died in 1834. She had brought him up from the age of three, when his mother died.

Others buried here include Archibald Constable (publisher), William Blackwood (bookseller), Professor John Playfair (mathematician) and Thomas Hamilton (architect). Many cordiners (shoe-makers) and brewers were also buried here.

Before Waterloo Place could be completed, the road had to be taken through part of the Old Calton Burying Ground. Great pains were taken to identify relatives of those whose graves would be affected, to seek permission to remove the bodies to the New Calton Burying Ground, to the south of Regent Road. These remains were all covered with white cloths and removed to their new resting-places in 1817. The ground was sited so as to be out of view from the houses in Regent Terrace, not yet built. A guard-tower was built in the middle, for the resident watchman to prevent the theft of bodies for sale to the medical school.

## Buildings in Waterloo Place

Part of each side of Waterloo Place was taken up by the triumphal arches of Regent Bridge. The eastern end of the road had no room for buildings because of the walls of the burying-ground which were faced with columns and niches.

A Mr Peter Lorimer offered a large sum of money in 1817 for the ground to the east of the North Bridge, and he undertook to build some houses. He also secured the contract to build a new Post Office in Waterloo Place. By 1820 he complained of difficulties in selling his buildings because of the state of the road which was still being built, although it was usable.

Waterloo Place contained a mixture of public buildings, commercial premises, taverns and private dwellings. One of the first buildings, in 1819, was at the eastern extremity on the north side, forming the corner with Calton Hill. This was the Calton Convening Rooms, used for meetings of the Incorporated Trades of Calton. The feu charter of the building restricted its use to a public building, not to be converted into shops or dwelling houses. The Calton Rooms were also used by a dancing instructor, by a Sunday School for Trinity College Church congregation and by the Edinburgh Choral Union. In 1820 the Feast of St Crispin was celebrated there, when 600 members of the Ancient Corporation of Cordiners (shoe-makers) marched there from Holyrood. By 1876 the building was also used by the Evangelical Union Church. In 1888 the Calton Rooms were converted into the Lands Valuation Office, later becoming the Burgh Assessor's Office and then the Edinburgh Corporation Water Department. In recent years it has been a restaurant.

## Hotels

On the north side of the street to the east of Regent Bridge, the Waterloo Hotel was built in 1819 and opened in 1821, the landlord being Charles Oman, a former tavern-boy. The hotel was the largest of its kind in Edinburgh, no other hotel having room to entertain more than fifty people. The coffee-room and dining-room each measured eighty feet by forty feet. The first guests to be entertained there were French officers who were visiting the city. It closed in 1897.

By 1833, in addition to the Waterloo Hotel, there were three taverns as well as an inn attached to the Regent coffee-house at no.14. John Rampling was then the proprietor of the Royal Saloon, incorporating a coffee-house and tavern at the western end of the north side. Rampling's Hotel was soon opened on the east side of the Waterloo Hotel into which it later merged.

The first temperance hotel opened to the west of the Waterloo Hotel in the 1850s. This became Darling's Regent Hotel in 1863. It was noted, not only for the absence of alcohol, but also for the prayer meetings held for guests every evening. In the 1920s, the hotel was a popular place for weddings, with an awning over the pavement. After a hundred years Darling's Hotel was bought by the North British Trust Hotels Group and licensed. It closed in 1976.

The New Waverley Temperance Hotel was at no.18, next to the burying ground, from the mid 1870s for over fifty years.

None of the hotels had many residents and must have been used mainly for drinking or as eating-houses. At the 1841 census there were eight men residents in Rampling's Hotel, with fifteen resident servants (five male and ten female), probably partly employed to serve non-resident guests. The inn at no.14 had no resident guests but four male and seven female resident servants while a commercial lodging house at no.17 had six lodgers. Even the Waterloo Hotel had only three visitors resident in 1861 and five in 1881.

## Post Office and Stamp Office

The Post Office moved from the corner of the North Bridge and the High Street in 1822 to the south side of Waterloo Place, east of Regent Bridge. Sir Edward Lees, who was for forty-five years Secretary to the Post Office in Scotland, had his home within it. Others who also lived there in 1841 were a watchman, a clerk and a messenger-porter with his wife, two daughters and grandchildren. By 1861 the accommodation was occupied by an inspector of letter-carriers and his family and in 1881 by a male housekeeper and his wife and children, two of whom were also Post Office employees.

At the Post Office mail was sorted in a room thirty feet square, deliberately kept dark so that letters could be examined by candling, that

The Post Office in about 1830.

is, holding them up to a light to see if they contained more than the one sheet allowed. The Post Office became busier over the next forty years, especially with the introduction of the penny post in 1840, Post Office orders for the transmission of money and the new Post Office savings bank. The number of employees increased from thirty in 1822 to 300 in 1858 and a new site was found at the south west end of Waterloo Place. This necessitated the demolition of the Theatre Royal and adjoining houses in Shakespeare Square.

The Prince Consort laid the foundation stone of the new building in 1861, two months before his death. For the ceremony, the old Post Office was draped from top to bottom with decorations, while flags were hung from other buildings in Waterloo Place and in Princes Street, the Bridges and Leith Street. The letter-carriers, all clad for the first time in blue in lieu of their old scarlet, were drawn up in a double rank within the galleries which were crowded by a fashionable audience. The new Post Office was designed by Robert Matheson, and opened for business in 1866 and is today Edinburgh's Head Post Office. A post to which customers (especially military) could hitch their horses can still be seen on the pavement outside.

At the time of the 1914-18 War, the Post Office employed boy foot-messengers to deliver telegrams and express letters. The boys were provided with boots, leggings, a coat and a cape. They sat on benches, moving along until their turn came. Having reached the front position, a boy would be given three farthings payment, no matter what distance he had to walk,

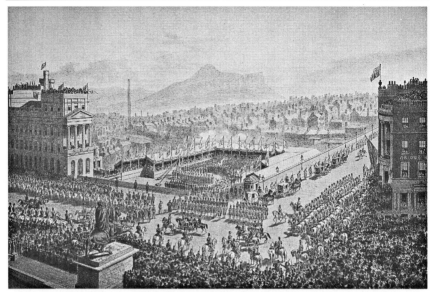

Prince Albert laying the foundation stone of the G.P.O. in 1861.
(*City Art Centre, Edinburgh*).

whether to St Andrew's Square or to Corstorphine, in order to deliver a
letter.

The old Post Office, which had meanwhile been used as a theatre, a hotel
and a popular rest-house for servicemen of the 1939-45 War, was used as an
annexe of the Post Office for twenty years from 1946. Only the ground floor
was used, as the upper floors had been seriously damaged in a spectacular
fire in the New Waverley Temperance Hotel in the late 1920s. The words
'Old Post Office' are still visible near the top of the facade. Since the 1970s
the building has been occupied by the Scottish Office, whose headquarters
are in St Andrews House nearby.

Also in 1822 the Stamp Office moved from Park Street to 10 Waterloo
Place. The Comptroller-General of Stamps and Taxes was Thomas Pender,
who had succeeded his father (of the same name) in the post. Thomas
Pender junior came from Salisbury Road to live nearer to his office: he had
four successive homes in Regent, Royal and Carlton Terraces between 1833
and 1843. A porter or a messenger lived in the premises of the Stamp Office,
the precursor of the Inland Revenue Department, which remained there
until well after the 1939-45 War.

## Art Exhibitions

Mr Bruce's gallery at 24 Waterloo Place, between the Waterloo Hotel and
the Convening Rooms, was used from 1820 for exhibitions of the Institution

for the Encouragement of Fine Arts in Scotland. The same premises, two large galleries, were used from 1827 to 1835 for the annual exhibitions of the new Scottish Academy (later to be Royal). Members of the hanging committee were provided with refreshments, mostly liquid, by Mr John Rampling, proprietor of the adjoining Royal Saloon. Halfway through the third annual exhibition the Academy accepted the offered loan of Rubens' *Adoration of the Shepherds*. However, the painting was too large to be taken up the stairs, so it was raised to the roof with block and tackle and lowered through the cupola, which had to be removed.

Below the galleries were the premises of Mr Davidson, a teacher of the Eastern District Academy. After the galleries closed, they were briefly used by the Edinburgh Select Subscription Library from 1837.

## Commercial Premises

Waterloo Place housed a variety of businesses, large and small. At the corner of Leith Street, Dickson's, seedsmen, remained for about ninety years. On the same side in 1833 were tea warehouses, trunk-makers, a tailor, a clothier, a bookseller and W R Chambers, publishers. Similar businesses were on the opposite side, and also coach-builders, musical instrument makers and a china warehouse. A perfumer, George Thomson, was at no.7 for over thirty years, followed by Miss E King, tobacconist.

Transport offices were much in evidence, starting with Scott's coach office in the 1830s, at which time the stage coach to London started its journey outside the Post Office. The General Steam Navigation Company was there from the 1850s to the 1880s. By the 1890s, no.7 housed many ocean-going businesses, including Cunard, P & O, the Anchor Line, the British India Steam Line, White Star Line, Dominion Line and booking offices for the Union Line, Castle Line and others. After a few years they had all moved elsewhere, to make way for William Sutherland, wine merchant at nos 3 and 5, to expand. Malcolm Urquhart's wine and spirit business then occupied nos 3, 5 and 7 for most of the first half of the twentieth century.

Other interesting occupiers were the Café Français et Restaurant at no.18 in the 1860s, followed there later by a gunpowder company. The Prince of Wales Operetta House was at no.23, later part of the Waterloo Hotel. The Edinburgh Gas Light Company came to no.25 in the 1850s and remained, under various names, for over a hundred years, with the result that the adjoining steep road up the Calton Hill became known as 'Gas Brae'.

Number 9 changed hands many times, from George Marshall, hosier, to Waddie and Company, manufacturing stationers, to Innes and Grieve, grocers, until the end of the nineteenth century when it became Carnegie and Beattie, restaurateurs, for some twenty years.

The undermentioned Houses are situate within the Boundaries of the

| Parish of | Quoad Sacra Parish of | Parliamentary Burgh of | Royal Burgh of | Town of | Village of |
|---|---|---|---|---|---|
| Saint Andrews | | Edinburgh | Edinburgh | | |

| No. of Schedule | HOUSES | | Name and Surname of each Person | Relation to Head of Family | Condition | Age of | | Rank, Profession, or Occupation | Where Born | Whether Blind, or Deaf and Dumb | No. of Children from 5 to 15 attending School | No. of Rooms with one or more Windows |
|---|---|---|---|---|---|---|---|---|---|---|---|---|
| | Road, Street, &c., and No. or Name of House | Uninhabited (U.), or Building (B.) / Inhabited | | | | Males | Females | | | | | |
| 1 | 6 Waterloo Pl. 1 | | James Currie | Head | Mar. | 50 | | Manager of School Revenue | Renfrew Abbey Shire | | 3 | 3 |
| | | | John Do | Son | Un. | 21 | | Compositor | " | | | |
| | | | Taylor Do | Dau. | Un. | | 17 | Works Helper | " | | | |
| | | | Robt. Do | Son | Un. | | 15 | Scholar | " | | | |
| | | | Lydella Do | Dau. | Un. | | 13 | Scholar | Middlothian Bonthill | | | |
| | | | Eliza Forsyne Do | Dau. | Un. | | 10 | | " | | | |
| | | | Mary Smith Do | Dau. | Un. | | 5 | | Edinburgh Register | | | |
| 2 | 10 Waterloo Pl. 1 | | William Balfour | Head | W. | 64 | | Boots Keeper | Clackmannan Alloa | | 8 | |
| | | | Gray Graham Do | Dau. | Un. | | 27 | | Lothian Edinburgh | | | |
| | | | John Buchanan Do | Dau. | Un. | | 25 | Scholar | Water Sleighhalge | | 1 | |
| | | | Lewis Do | Son | Nephew | Un. | 10 | | Scholar | Argyle Inveralie | | | |
| | | | Jane Buchanan Do | Niece | Un. | | 28 | | Argyle Inveralie | | | |
| | | | Eliza Mitchell | Husband | Un. | | 27 | Cook | Lothian Portobro | | | |
| | | | Jane Edwards Do | Servant | Un. | | 23 | Table Maid | Fife | | | |
| | | | John Ancaucke | Boarder | Un. | | 14 | Table Maid | Ruthie | | | |
| 3 | 14 Waterloo Pl. 1 | | Daniel Leonli | Head | Mar. | 34 | | Slate Master | St Andrews Cupar | | 15 | |
| | | | Margaret Do | Wife | | | 29 | | Edinburgh | | | |
| | | | Catherine Do | Daur. | Un. | | 4 | | | | | |
| | | | Margaret Wolf | Servant | Un. | | 16 | Praise servt. | Edinburgh Niece class | | | |
| | | | Margaret Mitchell | Servant | Un. | | 35 | Servt. | Edinburgh Midlothian | | | |
| | | | Williams Scotton | Servant | Un. | | 29 | Servt. Servt. | Surrey West Weddiham | | | |

| Total of Houses... 3 | Total of Males and Females... 6 / 15 | Total of School Children and Windowed Rooms... | 4 | 26 |
|---|---|---|---|---|

Extract of census return for 6, 10 and 14 Waterloo Place, 1861.

Caldwell Brothers, wholesale stationers, occupied 13, 15 and 17 for the second half of the nineteenth century and were succeeded by Andrew Craik, tobacconist, for many years.

The North British Railway (subsequently the London and North Eastern Railway) and the Forth Bridge Railway Company had their offices in part of the former Waterloo Hotel from 1898 for thirty years. The former had come from 2 and 8 Princes Street.

## Private Dwellings

Most of the residents of Waterloo Place were the proprietors or staff of commercial premises, with their families, but a few other people had their homes there. At the time of the 1841 census these included a teacher of drawing, a musician and a sempstress. At later censuses, residents were almost exclusively living at their places of work.

## Calton Jail

The Bridewell and House of Correction, designed by Robert Adam, were built on the site of the present St Andrew's House in 1791-95. The previous House of Correction had been in the Canongate. The Bridewell had 134 'sleeping-closets' each with a bed and a bible. There were fifty-two 'working parlours' or cages in which the prisoners were set to work for purposes of rehabilitation rather than punishment. There was a treadmill for hardened offenders and also a chapel. Some judges considered that the Bridewell trained offenders in crime: the openness of the working cells gave plenty of opportunity for this. Furthermore, some prisoners could talk out of the windows of their cells to people on Calton Hill.

While the Regent Bridge was under construction, a new prison building and the castellated and turreted Governor's House were built in 1815 to designs by Archibald Elliot. Lord Cockburn commented that 'it was a piece of undoubted bad taste to give so glorious an eminence to a prison'. Along the street was accommodation for turnkeys (warders). The new jail incorporated a school for illiterate prisoners. A number of French prisoners were confined in the jail from 1815 to 1817.

Jules Verne, in his recently discovered novel *Backwards to Britain*, based on his visit to Edinburgh in 1859, thought the prison resembled a miniature mediaeval town, perfectly clean as if waxed and polished.

On the roof was a platform for the execution of prisoners, watched by crowds on Calton Hill. A boy who was late for school after watching an execution wrote that 'after the interview with the headmaster of the Heriot School, I never wanted to see another'. A suggestion in the 1830s that the executions be on the hill itself was not adopted. The last public hanging, in

June 1864, was of George Bryce, a carter convicted of the murder of a nursemaid in a villa at Ratho. It was watched by a crowd of more than 20,000.

One of the first executions that was not public was of Eugene Chantrelle who had murdered his wife by gas poisoning in 1878. On the eve of his execution he asked the governor for three bottles of champagne and a whore. History does not relate whether his requests were granted. Others subsequently executed in the prison included two Gorebridge miners, Innes and Vickers, for the murder of a gamekeeper at Rosebery in 1884 and Jessie King in 1889, who was hanged for the murder of three illegitimate children who had been placed in her care.

The last prisoner to be executed in the prison was Philip Murray, in 1923. He had been convicted of murder after finding a man in his wife's bedroom and pushing the man through a top flat window. A resident of Calton Hill remembers the customary black flag being hoisted on the Governor's House. At some time after that, the door of the condemned cell was set up in the Ritz Picture House in Rutland Square, to lend colour to gangster pictures being shown. The graves of ten murderers are sealed under what is now the carpark for St Andrew's House.

To the east of the Bridewell was a debtors' prison. William Brown spent a week there in 1859 for non-payment of the Annuity Tax, levied for the payment of ministers' stipends. He published an account of his time there, where he occupied a white-painted cell twelve feet by nine feet, furnished with an iron bed, a chair and a table. He was allowed to commission a warder to buy food for him: the prisoners socialised in the kitchen. As soon as news of his arrest had spread, he had visits from his wife and from 'an

Calton Jail: the Debtors' prison (left), the Bridewell and House of Correction.

uninterrupted throng of friends'. He was the last annuity tax victim, as a riot in the streets had prevented any further arrests.

According to census returns there were 500 prisoners in all in 1841 (rather more male than female). The men were mainly artisans, such as flesher, mason, watchmaker, hatter, shoemaker, bookseller and blacksmith. The women were either domestic servants or in no occupation. The youngest prisoners were a boy and two girls aged nine, the girls being among the eleven females in the Lock-up House. Ten years later the number of prisoners had dropped to 450, of whom 320 were men: the youngest were a boy and girl aged twelve. For the rest of the nineteenth century there were about 300 prisoners, the number of women dropping to seventy in 1891.

Some prison staff lived in the prison: in 1841 they were four matrons, eight warders and two watchmen, the number of warders increasing to twelve by 1891. In 1851 the prison hospital had a resident physician, house surgeon and medical pupil attending thirteen patients, but the hospital was not mentioned in any other census.

Towards the end of the nineteenth century a nine-year-old boy, George Baird, who lived in Greenside, delivered milk to the jail, going through many doors which each had to be unlocked and relocked as he passed through. The prisoners provided a service to the public by taking in washing which was returned beautifully laundered.

One of the last to be imprisoned in the jail was Manny (later Lord) Shinwell, who spent five months there in 1919 for taking part in Glasgow riots protesting at the unemployment facing demobbed soldiers. Calton Jail was closed in 1924 and the prisoners transferred to Saughton Prison.

Calton Jail: the City and County Jail (the Felons' Prison), with the Governor's House behind.

## *Governor's House*

It is not uncommon for overseas visitors to assume that the Governor's House, built like a baronial castle on the top of a precipitous rock, is Edinburgh Castle.

Successive governors or captains of the jail lived in this house. The first was James Young, who was resident by 1823, followed by Lieut. H Rose who was governor of the County Jail but not of the Bridewell, where J Kirkwood was in charge. By 1841 the posts had been amalgamated and John Smith lived in the house for over thirty years with his wife and mother-in-law and brought up seven young children there. Capt.James Christie then took over for more than twenty years, having six children. Around the turn of the century a more senior officer was appointed as governor, Lt.Col.John Campbell, who was succeeded by Major W Stewart. From the windows of the house the Governor could keep a watchful eye on the prisoners' exercise yards behind the prison.

After the prison closed, the Governor's House was left empty and its condition deteriorated until quite recently when the Scottish Office took it over.

## *Royal High School*

By the nineteenth century, the old Royal High School buildings in Infirmary Street were becoming overcrowded with classes of about 200 boys. A new site was sought which would be accessible to families living in the New Town and beyond. The first site to be considered was at Canonmills but that was then used for building the Edinburgh Academy. The North Loch (now West Princes Street gardens) was rejected because the inhabitants of Princes Street would be certain to object. The city commissioned Thomas Hamilton, a former pupil of the school, to design a new school in St Andrew Square, but the Royal Bank of Scotland acquired that site. Finally the ground to the south of Calton Hill was chosen, on the newly built Regent Road. This was described by the Town Council as 'the only place in the New Town now left to which the High School can with any propriety be removed'.

At the laying of the foundation stone in 1825, the masters and boys processed from Infirmary Street, each boy carrying a peeled willow-rod.

Members of the public were invited to subscribe but a contemporary observer was doubtful whether enough would be promised. He wrote, in December 1825:

The subscription for the new High School has fairly commenced, our magistrates and council taking the lead. At least £10,000 will be required besides the

The Royal High School and Burns Monument, from a watercolour by Thomas Hamilton, RSA, 1784–1858 (*National Gallery of Scotland*).

proceeds of the old school, and if they trust to what is to be got by hanging up subscription papers in banking houses and the like, I fear it will be long before the building is commenced.

In the event, the public subscribed only £4,000.

The new school was formally opened in 1829, with 700 boys present as well as 'magistrates, professors, clergy and many ladies and gentlemen filling every corner of it'. In the evening the event was celebrated with a dinner for 400 at the Waterloo Hotel.

## Rectors

The Rector at the time of the school's removal to Regent Road was Dr Aglionby Ross Carson. Three months before his appointment he had declined the offer of the chair of Greek at St Andrews University, to which he had been elected although not a candidate. He was succeeded in 1845 by Dr Leonard Schmitz, who came to live in Carlton and then Regent Terrace.

## Rector's Salary

James Colston (later a bailie) wrote an open letter to the Lord Provost in 1863 pointing out that the Rector's salary was £200 p.a. and that of each of the four classics masters was £140. Capitation allowances and class fees were added to salaries. Fees paid by the boys had remained unchanged since 1827 at £1.5.0. per quarter for the Rector's class and £1 for the other four classes. Pensions were wholly or partly paid by levying a tax on new teachers. Colston was concerned that High School teachers were paid less than those of Edinburgh Academy. Dr Schmitz, the Rector, told the education committee that his income largely depended on the abilities of the other masters, on whose appointments he had no say. His own pupils came from the fourth class where the numbers depended on the popularity and efficiency of their master. The education committee decided that there was no need even to discuss whether the Rector should have a voice in the appointment of masters since there was then no vacancy.

## Other Buildings

The school janitor had his home in the western lodge, which became a swimming bath in 1885 and then a classroom. The present janitor's lodge was built in 1885. In 1861 the then janitor, Donald Sinclair, had an unmarried daughter living with him who kept a 'shop to supply the Royal High School'.

Wooden huts were erected in the playground in the 1920s to house some preparatory and junior classes until a new site was ready at Jock's Lodge. A boarding house was acquired in 1927 at 24 Royal Terrace, under the care of Mr and Mrs D H M Dawson. Successive house-masters were in charge until the boarding house was no longer required, when the school moved to Barnton.

## Proposed Extension of School Buildings

Overcrowding of the school buldings led to the school acquiring no.1 Regent Terrace in 1945 and, soon afterwards, nos 2 and 4 to be used as classrooms. Number 1 was adapted for use by art classes whose pupils had been meeting at Regent Road School.

In 1958 the education committee discussed the possibility of acquiring four acres of the private Regent, Royal and Carlton Terraces Gardens, but this was strenuously opposed by the proprietors of the gardens. In the following year the committee approved an alternative plan to build an extension of the school on the south side of Regent Road, with a connecting tunnel. A year later, that plan was abandoned and a new plan was approved to place the extension between the existing school and the houses of Regent Terrace.

Eventually, in July 1961, the proposal to build a new school at Barnton was accepted and the Royal High School moved there in 1968. The old buildings were then adapted to house a future Scottish Parliament which did not materialise. The Crown Office is now in the old Royal High School.

## Royal Visitors to the School

The Prince of Wales (later King Edward VII) took up residence in the Palace of Holyroodhouse for two months in 1859 while receiving tuition from the Rector of the Royal High School, Dr Leonard Schmitz. His brother, the Duke of Edinburgh, followed him three years later.

Three French princes attended the school in 1859-60. They were His Royal Highness Ferdinand d'Orléans, Duc d'Alençon; HRH Louis d'Orléans, Prince de Condé and HRH Pierre d'Orléans, Duc de Penthièvre.

King Edward VII, accompanied by Queen Alexandra, revisited the school in 1903 and the next Prince of Wales (later King Edward VIII) visited in 1919. On a visit by Crown Prince Hirohito of Japan in 1921 the school choir sang the Japanese national anthem, being the first time that the Crown Prince (later Emperor) had heard it sung in this country.

State Procession of King Edward VII and Queen Alexandra, 1903.

## *The Burns Monument*

A monument to Robert Burns was built in 1831 on the south side of Regent Road, opposite the entrance to Regent Terrace. It was designed by Thomas Hamilton in the style of a circular Greek temple. A life-size white marble statue of the poet by Flaxman was placed inside but it became blackened by fumes from the gas works below it. After fifteen years the statue was removed to the hall of the University Library; in 1861 it was moved to the Scottish National Gallery and again, in 1889, to the Scottish National Portrait Gallery entrance hall, where it could be better seen.

In 1833 a public appeal was launched to make good the deficit on the monument, which was enclosed by a parapet, wall and rail, with shrubbery around.

The monument was opened to the public in 1863. Over the next three years 14,000 people visited it, nearly half of them leaving their names in a visitors' book, a few coming from the USA and Canada. One visitor added a comment: 'pity that one of nature's nobles should have been connected with such a hellish trade', referring, presumably, to Burns's employment as an excise officer.

Throughout the 1860s over a hundred relics of Burns were collected and displayed until 1901, when the museum was removed because of damp, first to the City Chambers Museum, together with its curator John Jack, and then to Lady Stair's House.

The monument was closed to the public from 1901 to 1960, when it became the headquarters of the Edinburgh and District Burns Club.

## St Andrew's House

Discussions about the need for the Scottish Office to have one centralised building in Edinburgh started in 1912, when Lord Pentland was Secretary of State for Scotland. A plan was prepared for building on the site of the Calton Jail, but a proposed architectural competition for a design was shelved during the 1914-18 War.

The prison was vacated in 1925 and the Army Council gained permission for the buildings to be used as the headquarters of Scottish Command, which were then in the *Scotsman* building. However, plans for conversion were rejected as being too costly, and Sir John Gilmour, Secretary of State, pressed his needs because of the inconvenience of his departments being spread over eighteen buildings in Edinburgh. In 1928 it was agreed that the site of the jail could accommodate the Scottish Office and the War Office staff, with one wing for a new Sheriff Court (then at the north end of George IV Bridge). The Sheriff Court was subsequently built in the High Street.

During many protracted negotiations about alternative schemes and the choice of architect, the Cockburn Association commissioned a scheme in 1933 to use Regent Terrace as an alternative site for the Scottish Office, echoing the general grouping of Playfair's terrace with bolder projections and with an assembly hall and a colossal tower at the east end. Carlton Terrace could have been used for a future extension. Luckily, that scheme came to nothing. One member of the City Engineer's department claimed that 'St Andrew's House was designed in the correspondence columns of the *Scotsman*!'.

Meanwhile, the Scottish Office had grown considerably and any scheme on the Calton site would have had to omit any accommodation for the War Office or for other departments.

Finally, a selection committee appointed Thomas Smith Tait in 1934 as architect for the new Scottish Office. The Duke of Gloucester laid the foundation stone in 1937 and the building was completed in 1939 and named St Andrew's House. The title 'Scottish Whitehall' had been rejected. Staff moved in during September and October of that year. There was no official opening ceremony because of the outbreak of war, but King George VI and Queen Elizabeth made an official visit in February 1940. The King then drew out of his pocket the gold key, intended for the official opening, and handed it to the Secretary of State for Scotland saying, 'You'd better have this'.

## Transport

Horse tramcars, introduced in 1871, were replaced by cable cars, of which the last one from the GPO to Portobello ran in 1922. A small piece of the old cable track can still be seen in the middle of the road at the west end of Waterloo Place, showing two rails and the centre slot which carried the gripper. From 1923 to 1956 electric trams ran eastwards from Waterloo Place.

After the start of the 1914–18 War an open tram used as a recruitment car stood in Waterloo Place and huge queues formed of young men eager to enlist. When troops marched into town from Piershill Barracks, residents flocked to cheer them shouting encouraging remarks such as 'I'll bake a cake for you when you come back for Christmas'.

Horses and cabs were available for hire on the south side of Waterloo Place. Some of the cab stances can today be identified by the brass letters on the edge of the kerbstones, CS3, CS4 and CS5.

## Trees

William Stark, the architect who in 1814 had emphasised the importance of trees, would have been pleased to know that trees were planted in the roadway along the south side of Regent Road in 1895, sixteen years after the idea had been mooted by the Cockburn Association. Trees remained there for about seventy years.

# 3.
# REGENT TERRACE

William Playfair's plan for Regent Terrace, dated 1825, shows his frontage for the whole terrace. Taking account of the slope of the hill, he planned the houses in groups of six, each house in a group having progressively one more step up to the front door. He planned a large town house, double the size of all the others, at the western end of the terrace, but this house never materialised and two houses were built on the site. For this reason, all other houses were renumbered in 1833 by the addition of one digit. The revised numbering is used in the following account.

Stances for these houses had already been advertised in February 1824, for feuing two months later, and Playfair's plan named all the feuars, most of whom were builders. Building soon began and in June 1825 an observer recorded that 'On the south-east side of the Calton Hill there will soon be a long range of houses if we may judge by the extent of the foundations digging'. A year later he wrote 'The Regent Terrace, where twelve months ago there were only foundations digging now presents us with seventeen houses nearly complete besides six lately begun'.

The first recorded meeting of the feuars of Regent Terrace and Carlton Place (later Carlton Terrace) took place on 28 March 1825 within MacRitchie, Bayley and Henderson's Chambers. Subsequent meetings were held in the more convivial atmosphere of the Ship Tavern, Register Street. Mr William Henry, builder, was chairman of meetings of feuars from 1825 for at least ten years, and the committee then voted a sum for a piece of silver plate to be presented to him. He was the feuar of seven stances in Regent Terrace, but never lived there.

The eighteen feuars had 'waited upon Mr Playfair relative to the alteration proposed on the approach to the Terrace from the West and as to the level and line of the Terrace itself. ...Mr Playfair in the most handsome manner agreed to consider the propriety of raising the small road and widening the pleasure ground'. That referred to what later became known as the Front Bank garden, between Regent Road and Regent Terrace, for the proposal was for 'the first line of the house at the eastern end to be kept ten feet farther back from the Regent Road than originally proposed, the west end remaining at the same distance as before'.

Early meetings were chiefly concerned with estimates for building the retaining wall of the front bank garden and for the construction of Regent Road to the west of Regent Terrace. In 1829 the feuars were to sue the Town Council for not completing the road past the new Royal High School: they were also insisting on a foot pavement along the front of the High School. By 1840 the Town Council was still reluctant to pay for this pavement.

## Houses and House Prices

Houses were not built in any particular order, but frontages had to conform to Playfair's plan. Inside, feuars were free to vary the lay-out, so that houses were similar but not identical. A single house was built on each stance but in 1835 the gardens committee threatened legal proceedings to prevent Andrew Ferris, a builder, making a common stair on any of his stances. Prices were probably similar to the £1,500 paid to David Chalmers, a baker, in 1831 for no.6, which was sold in 1877 for £2,700. Number 3 was let for £40 per six months in 1839 to George Munro by Bailie Robert Wright, an architect and a terraces feuar from 1825.

The west end of Regent Terrace.

## University Principal

In 1826 no.13 was the first house to be occupied, where the owner was Isaac Bayley, SSC (a Solicitor to the Supreme Courts). In the following year he was joined by his father-in-law, the Very Rev. George Husband Baird.

Dr Baird was Principal of Edinburgh University from 1793 until his death in 1840, and was simultaneously Minister of the new North parish church, later known as West St Giles, from 1799 to 1840. Dr Baird married Isabella, the eldest daughter of Thomas Elder of Forneth, Lord Provost of Edinburgh for three terms of two years each, between 1788 and 1798. They had two sons and three daughters. After his wife's death he left Ramsay Lodge (built for Allan Ramsay, the poet, and known as Goosepie Lodge) to live with his daughter and son-in-law, Marion and Isaac Bayley.

George Baird had been through university without graduating, and was awarded an honorary MA in 1787 'as one who had been many years an alumnus'. He was appointed Principal of the University at the early age of thirty-two, having previously been Professor of Oriental Languages for one year at the same time as being Minister of New Greyfriars. He owed his rapid promotion to the influence of his father-in-law, the Lord Provost.

In addition to his oriental languages, he had an exceptional knowledge of all the living languages of Europe, but his only publication was a sermon which 'was in the act of going through the press but stopt after 48 pages had been thrown off', in 1795.

As University Principal, Dr Baird was annoyed that the University Librarian had an official house, while he did not. Furthermore, Dr Baird did not actually wish to live in College 'from the annoyance of the concourse of students every hour of the day' but magnanimously said he was prepared to sacrifice his private feelings to the interest of the University.

During his Principalship, student numbers increased from 1,000 to 2,000, and the building of Old College was completed. It was badly needed, for in 1810 twenty-four professors shared eleven rooms, with two of them having to teach by candle-light even at midday.

Principal Baird's kindliness, cheerfulness, deferential manners and conversational powers won for him the respect of the Senatus and of the Town Council. Preaching about the mental condition of the king, 'he shed so many tears that it was said his sermon might have been described as "From George Husband Baird to George III – greeting"'.

Dr Baird was Moderator of the General Assembly of the Church of Scotland in 1800 and was the founder and first convener of the General Assembly's Highlands and Islands committee. In 1825 the General Assembly gave sanction to his scheme for the education of the poor of the highlands and islands, especially for the neglected Celtic race.

Though advanced in years, he travelled no fewer than seven thousand miles in the interests of this work, affirming that he had found nearly one hundred thousand human beings unable either to read or write and innumerable districts where the people could not hear a sermon above once a year, and had seen thousands of habitations where a Sabbath bell was never heard, where he had now witnessed schools and libraries established, knowledge increased and greedily received. (Fasti).

His daughter and son-in-law continued to live in their house for many years and their son George returned to live there after his parents' death. Father and son were each able to afford five living-in servants.

## *Other Early Residents*

No other residents came to the terrace until 1829, when five more houses were occupied, nos 8, 15, 16, 27 and 34. These new occupiers were, respectively, Robert Mitchell (wine merchant), John Hamilton Colt of Gartsherrie, John Easton (physician), John MacFie (sugar refiner) and Major William Yule of the Honourable East India Company Service (HEICS).

Major Yule brought his family to no.34. He had retired from the HEICS in 1806 with a valuable collection of Persian and Arabic manuscripts which was later presented to the British Museum by his sons.

He had three sons who had distinguished careers in India. The eldest was Sir George Yule, KCSI, CB: during the mutiny, with a corps of mounted European volunteers, he drove out large bodies of the mutineers and kept open the navigation of the Ganges. He subsequently became Chief Commissioner of Oudh, Political Resident at Hyderabad and a Member of the Council of India.

Another son was Sir Henry Yule, KCSI, CB, the celebrated geographer. As a pupil at the High School he showed considerable ingenuity but with more liking for Greek plays and German than for mathematics. In India, his intense interest in history and archaeology led to many publications, the most important being his edition of Marco Polo, which earned him the founder's medal of the Royal Geographical Society.

A new resident in 1830 was Alexander Russell, tea, wine and spirit merchant at 17. The anonymous diarist reported in July 1831 that the terrace was very nearly completed. By 1833 all the houses were occupied except for no.14.

The only original feuar to live in Regent Terrace was Lewis Alexander Wallace, architect, who feued the four most easterly stances and came to live in the last house (34) in 1839, with his wife and six sons and four daughters, having previously rented out his house for ten years to Major Yule. By the time of the 1861 census he was a widower and his four daughters were still unmarried and living with him, while his sons had left home. The family had always had four women domestic servants, to whom were added a butler and a footman by 1861.

In the early days of Regent Terrace, several houses were used as town houses by families whose country seat was their main home. One such resident was John Hamilton Colt of Gartsherrie, who had been brought up by his great-aunt Janet, the last Countess of Hyndford, after his parents had died when he was nine. He became the owner of estates in Scotland and England with a town house at 15 Regent Terrace from 1829 in which year he sent to the Chancellor of the Exchequer a scheme for paying off the £80 millions of debt owed by the nation. His scheme was partially adopted but his authorship was not publicly acknowledged. Colt started a refuge for the destitute in Edinburgh and was also responsible for the first railway in Scotland in 1823, a stretch of seven miles between Kirkintilloch and his home at Gartsherrie. This later became part of the North British Railway's main line to the north.

One of his eight children died young before he came here, and one shortly after his arrival. His son Charles, who came to the terrace at the age of nine, was with Sir Walter Gilbert during his memorable two days ride in pursuit of Shere-Singh and the subsequent capture and surrender of that great chief in the Sikh rebellion in the 1850s.

## French Royal Family

The highest-born resident was the Duc d'Angoulême, son of Charles X of France, the last of the Bourbons. In October 1830, following a revolution which brought Louis Philippe to the throne, the king arrived at Leith by sea and lived in exile in the Palace of Holyroodhouse for nearly two years. He brought with him a suite of 100, many of whom lodged in the Canongate.

The king's elder son, the Duc d'Angoulême, who had resigned his rights to the crown, came by land to Edinburgh with his wife. The duke and duchess moved into what was then 21 and is now 22 Regent Terrace and spent the winter there, until apartments were prepared for them in Holyrood.

Charles X also brought with him his ten-year-old grandson, the Duc de Bordeaux, Henri Charles Ferdinand Dieudonné d'Artois, in whose favour he had abdicated. The prince's father, the Duc de Berri, had been assassinated. A contemporary newspaper reported that the Duchesse de Berri was about to move into another house in Regent Terrace in November 1830.

The young prince, a slender, fair-haired boy, used to visit his uncle and aunt in Regent Terrace and an engraving by Newton shows him wearing the

The Duchesse d'Angoulême, daughter of Louis XVI and Marie Antoinette, 1796, by Feodor Bogalevitch. (*In the collection of the Duke of Buccleuch and Queensberry KT*).

Stewart tartan, and with his dog, in the gardens there. In spite of being lame because of an old ankle injury, he was often seen in a blue waisted coat and a beret – the latter an unusual headgear in Scotland – on Calton Hill, taking long walks with his tutor, until fear of assassination at the hands of some French 'constitutionalists' made public places dangerous. The boy made his first communion at St Mary's Roman Catholic Cathedral in February 1832 and presented a monstrance, which is still in use.

The Duc d'Angoulême was childless, and was said to be sickly and morose and a political nonentity. His wife, the daughter of Louis XVI and Marie Antoinette, was as silent and sorrowful as her husband, but was willing to make any sacrifice for her husband's Bourbon family. However, Napoleon had described her as 'the only man in the family'. After moving to Holyrood, the duke and duchess were frequently seen arm-in-arm, walking in the Canongate and High Street, 'he dressed in an old blue great-coat and she enveloped in a coat or mantle which was not much superior in appearance'.

On sailing from Leith on 18 September 1832, en route for Austria, the young Duke of Bordeaux wept bitterly at the thought of leaving Scotland, to which he had become warmly attached.

## *Ministers of the Church*

A few ministers lived here at some distance from their churches. Unless they had private means, they must surely have had difficulties in living in such large houses on their stipends.

The Rev. John McGilchrist lived at 30 Regent Terrace for twenty-three years from 1831 until he moved to George Street. He was the United Presbyterian Minister of Rose Street chapel. In 1851, five of his seven children were living at home, the eldest being sixteen (the other two may have died in infancy). He and his wife also had a medical student and a divinity student as boarders, and only one servant, perhaps indicating that they were hard up.

The Rev. James Marshall was minister of the Tolbooth during his five years from 1832 at no.4, followed by one year at 16. With five sons and three daughters, his house must have been noisy. He left Edinburgh on demitting his charge, having adopted views which led him to leave the Church of Scotland and take holy orders in the Church of England.

One of his sons, Sir James Marshall, spent his childhood here: he was prevented from going into the army because of the loss of his right arm in a gun accident. Instead, he took holy orders in 1854 but soon joined the Church of Rome and was a friend of Cardinal Newman. Thereafter he had a varied career, being first a classical teacher and later Chief Magistrate of the Gold Coast where, on the outbreak of the Ashanti War in 1874, he secured the chiefs' assent to the impressment of their tribesmen. He rose to become Chief Justice of the Gold Coast.

Another minister here at this time was the Rev. Dr John Hunter, who was appointed to the Tron Church in 1832 after a legal contest with the Kirk session was taken to the House of Lords. The dispute came about by a minority of the patrons challenging the Town Council's right to appoint a successor to the church. During his thirty-three years in the terrace, he lived in four different houses (12, 9, 15 and 2 – where he died at the age of seventy-seven).

## Scientific Craftsmen

Alexander Adie, FRS, who lived at number 10 from 1832 to 1838, was optician to William IV and to Queen Victoria and had premises at 58 Princes Street. He invented the sympiesometer or marine barometer and set up a small observatory long before a public observatory was opened. His daughter Helen married first James Marshall of Callander, and secondly Sir William Menzies WS, whose brother (and, earlier, grandfather) lived at 35 Royal Terrace.

William Home Lizars was originally a painter, a fellow-student of Sir David Wilkie. His best-known pictures, *Reading the Will* and *A Scottish Wedding* are now in the National Gallery of Scotland. He later became an engraver, perfecting a method of etching which performed all the functions of wood-engraving for his many book illustrations. As a map engraver, in 1839 he was an expert witness at the trial of the Earl of Stirling, who was his next-door neighbour in Carlton Terrace, where Lizars had moved after six years at 3 Regent Terrace.

## Solicitors

At the time of the 1841 census, six householders described themselves as independent (meaning that they lived on private means) and several of them had country houses. Four others were solicitors (as were sons of two of the country gentlemen).

One of the solicitors who lived here was George Munro, SSC, with his wife and five small children at no.3. In 1841, two years after his arrival, he had five servants, so his basement would have been fully occupied. Mr Munro discovered in 1850 that a forged cheque had been drawn on his account at the National Bank and that the savings accounts of his two young daughters had also been robbed of small sums. Suspicion fell on one of Mr Munro's clerks, absent from the office. A detective found that the suspect had changed his lodgings and had taken to drink – his friends said that he had 'gone with the quickness of a shot into this wild life', and they considered him mad. Eventually the detective traced him, 'bound to the easy-chair – not made for terror-ridden criminals, these rests ... his mouth gaped quite open so that I could even see his parched tongue, as it quivered like a touched jelly-fish'. The accused was found guilty of forgery and sentenced to fourteen years transportation.

## Royal High School Teachers

When the new Royal High School opened in 1829, three teachers took the opportunity to live a stone's throw from the school. They were George Lees at 9, William Pyper at 22 (later Professor of Humanity at St Andrews University) and Samuel Lindsay at 28, who published a slim volume entitled *High School Vocabulary* – not a list of words peculiar to the school, but a Latin-English vocabulary. Pyper appears to have let his house to the Duc d'Angoulême for six months. Lees was also, simultaneously, lecturer in mathematics and natural philosophy at the Watt Institute and School of Arts (later Heriot-Watt University) and at the Military and Naval Academy in Lothian Road.

The most distinguished High School teacher to live in the terrace was Dr Leonard Schmitz, Rector of the school from 1845 to 1866. Schmitz was born near Aix-la-Chapelle and lost his right arm in an accident at the age of twelve. He had put his arm between the spokes of the wheel of a steam engine to retrieve his cap which a friend had thrown there. He gained his PhD in Bonn where, in 1836, he married Eliza Mary Machell, a young English lady who had gone there to study German. He and his wife moved to Yorkshire, where he was a private tutor and he became a naturalised British subject.

After coming to Edinburgh they lived at 11 Carlton Terrace for seven years before moving to 9 Regent Terrace in 1852 until they left Edinburgh in 1866. In this last house, the Schmitzes took in two boys as boarders in addition to their own family of five sons and six daughters, with four resident servants.

In 1847 Dr Schmitz chaired a meeting of 600 to 700 Scottish teachers to establish the Educational Institute of Scotland, which set strict professional standards and improved the status of schoolmasters throughout Scotland. Schmitz told the meeting that teachers were treated little better than servants or menials, and that it was believed that a person good for nothing else was good enough to be a schoolmaster and that parents looked on schoolmasters as a sort of nurse for naughty children.

Dr Schmitz was a prolific historical writer and translator and he became a teacher of some eminence.

After retiring from the High School, Leonard Schmitz was appointed Principal of the London International College at Isleworth, 1866-74. In

1889 he had a severe accident in Portsmouth, after which his friends and former pupils (including the Prince of Wales) presented him with a testimonial of over £1,000.

Bailie James Colston, who had been concerned about the salaries of Dr Schmitz and other masters in the 1860s later came, as a widower, from Findhorn Place to 23 Regent Terrace, with his one-year-old daughter and his mother. He lived there for the last twenty-three years of his life until his death in 1897. As well as raising money for Edinburgh Royal Infirmary, which was then a voluntary hospital and dependant on contributions from the public, he raised large sums for the victims of national disasters such as a fire in Chicago and a famine in China. He was also the author of an important history of Edinburgh's water supply.

## Census Returns

Throughout the nineteenth century there was an average of three resident domestic servants in each house, though with considerable variation. The numbers of children showed far more fluctuation.

The 1841 census showed larger families than any other nineteenth century census. Although about one third of the houses were childless, there were seventy-two children under fifteen living in the terrace, including two families with seven young children. The thirty-four houses had, between them, 265 residents including ninety-seven domestic servants. Half that number of people lives in Regent Terrace today.

By 1851 the number of children had dropped sharply to twenty-six. That census gave more information about servants than that of 1841, as their occupations were defined. Practically every house had a resident cook and housemaid. Some had, additionally, a table maid, kitchen maid, laundress, nurse, nursery maid, lady's maid, butler or coachman. A laundress would have had the use of a laundry in the basement, fitted with a copper boiler, three large porcelain sinks and a mangle. Some houses still have these laundry fittings. There would also have been a number of non-resident servants such as gardeners, but these would not be listed in the census.

The Principal Extractor of the Court of Session, John Parker, living at no.2, had ten children and seven resident domestic servants in 1841, which must have led to logistical problems. But sometimes the domestic establishment was in inverse proportion to the family's apparent needs. In 1851 a 49-year-old widow with a seven-year-old daughter had five servants including a lady's maid, while a minister and his wife with five children aged four to sixteen and two university students as boarders had only one servant.

There were then ten 'independent' householders as well as six solicitors and five merchants (mostly wine and spirits).

## Lord Provost

Another large family was the Boyds at no.11 from 1846. Sir Thomas Jamieson Boyd was the first resident to become Lord Provost, although he had left the terrace before reaching that position. His brother was already living in Royal Terrace.

Sir Thomas was senior partner in the publishing firm of Oliver and Boyd and at the 1861 census he described himself as a master publisher, employing fifty-six men, twenty-two boys, thirty-seven women and ten girls. At that time he also had three sons and six daughters, necessitating a domestic complement of eight resident servants.

He was three times Master of the Merchant Company and promoted a scheme whereby the four 'hospitals' or orphanages were converted into day schools. Sir Thomas endowed a chair at Edinburgh University to complete the commercial side of the education provided by Merchant Company schools, a scheme which was then used as a model in England. Among his philanthropic activities he established industrial schools for neglected Edinburgh children.

He was, perhaps, best known for his part in establishing the new Edinburgh Royal Infirmary. He was chairman of the committee responsible for raising money for the hospital and it was fitting that in 1879 he performed the opening ceremony of it, since no member of the Royal family was available. After the public ceremony, nearly 40,000 people took the opportunity to inspect the hospital, when the wards and corridors were specially illuminated. Two days later, 240 patients were brought by cabs and other conveyances from the old to the new Infirmary.

Sir Thomas was knighted by Queen Victoria at the time of the 1881 Review of Volunteers in Holyrood Park, dubbed 'the wet review' on account of the relentless rain.

## President of the Royal Scottish Academy

By 1861 the three occupations most frequently listed in the census were solicitor, merchant and minister, to whom were added a distinguished artist, Sir George Harvey, President of the Royal Scottish Academy, who came to 21 as a widower in 1854 and lived there till he died in 1876. His two daughters continued to occupy the house until the middle of the Great War.

Sir George Harvey was one of the founders of the RSA and was elected President in 1864 and knighted in 1867. His reputation was made by his large historical canvases, especially of scenes showing lives of the Covenanters. His painting *Quitting the Manse* showed a minister and his family who had to give up their home after the Disruption.

After his death one of his daughters wrote that after sixteen years in lodgings, he had appreciated the joys of his own home in Regent Terrace. He had been twice widowed, but had a very happy old age. He spent quiet Sundays in the garden, reading. He also enjoyed brisk morning walks to Arthur's Seat and Salisbury Crags, but his idea of the acme of comfort was to sit with his slippers off, toasting his feet within the fender.

Sir George always dined at half past four and, being very hospitable, liked to serve his guests himself. He loved children and enjoyed entertaining them in his house, sometimes playing charades. On his way home along the terrace, he would often find his way barred by some child demanding his attention. He conducted family worship every evening, and held the office of deacon in the St Augustine Church.

## Bishop of Edinburgh

A few doors away from Harvey lived an unusual figure in the person of the Right Rev. Charles Hughes Terrot, DD, FRSE, who was Bishop of Edinburgh from 1841 and Primus of Scotland from 1857. As bishop he operated from St Paul's, York Place, where he had been junior minister and then rector. The episcopal cathedral of St Mary's had not yet been built. Grant (1882) wrote 'his quaint little figure, with shovel-hat and knee-breeches, was long familiar in the streets of Edinburgh'.

Bishop Terrot was born in Cuddalore only a few weeks before his father's death at the siege of Bangalore. His appearance was said to be gentle, placid, almost feminine. His sarcastic powers enabled him to deliver a snub with the least possible offence. When asked to preside at an examination of an ecclesiastical school of whose principles he did not entirely approve, he replied, 'I like a scholar and I like a good dinner, but I don't like to frequent the places where either are being prepared'. He used to say that the two chief impediments to good conversation were humbug and humdrum. He detested what he called 'pious twaddle' and disliked being called Lord Bishop.

Terrot was twice married. His first wife died after thirty-seven years of marriage; they had fourteen children, six of whom pre-deceased him. His eldest daughter Sarah Anne accompanied Florence Nightingale to the Crimea and was later decorated by Queen Victoria at Balmoral with the Royal Red Cross. She kept a journal, published more than a hundred years later as *Nurse Sarah Anne*, with vivid accounts of, first, the terrifying ordeal of the sea journey through storms which left the nurses sick and exhausted in cabins which were unventilated, unlit and awash with sea water. She wrote of the appalling conditions in the two hositals at Scutari which were grossly under-staffed and under-equipped and where men died like flies.

The bishop, who had earlier lived in Northumberland Street, remarried in 1859 and came to his second wife's home at 26 Regent Terrace, where she

Charles Hughes Terrot, Bishop of Edinburgh, a resident of Regent Terrace. (*Modern Athenians*).

had lived with each of her two previous husbands. She was twenty-six years younger than he was, but she died in 1862 aged only forty-five. She had always had plenty of help in looking after her large house; at the 1851 census, as a widow, she had a butler, a cook, a lady's maid, a housemaid and a kitchen maid. Ten years later, as Mrs Terrot, she had five female domestic servants, whose precise occupations were unspecified. In the year of her death, the bishop had a stroke which partially paralysed him and he resigned all his appointments and moved to Carlton Street, where he died in 1872, aged eighty-one.

## Master of the Merchant Company

A young man who lived with his uncle, James Marshall, at 15 Regent Terrace from 1865 was John Cowan, whose place of birth was given in the 1871 census as 'Atlantic Ocean': his father was a missionary in Jamaica. At the age of twenty-six he was an iron merchant and already an employer of twenty-six boys and thirty men. He went on to become the Chairman of Redpath, Brown and Co, steel constructional engineers, and Master of the Merchant Company. He was knighted in 1915.

Two incidents illustrate that Sir John was much loved by his employees. In 1906, he stood for Edinburgh Town Council and some groundless aspersions were cast on his character. His workers showed their support for him by marching four abreast through the streets of Edinburgh, with a band at their head. And in 1920, five hundred of his workers invited Sir John and Lady Cowan to a dinner to commemorate the diamond jubilee of his connection with the firm. The menu was good plain fare, and included tomato soup, fried filleted haddock with anchovy sauce, beefsteak pie and plum pudding.

## A Popular Professor

The various academics who came to live in the terrace practically all came after they had been appointed to university chairs.

Apart from Principal Baird, the first academic to live here was David Masson, who was Professor of Rhetoric and English Literature at Edinburgh University for thirty years from 1865. At the end of his life he was Historiographer Royal for Scotland for twelve years.

Masson had spent three years in Edinburgh studying for the Church but changed his mind during the stir of the Disruption. From 1853 he was Professor of English Literature in University College, London. While there, he married the eighteen-year-old Emily Rosaline Orme. After coming to live in Edinburgh in 1865 their first home was in Rosebery Crescent, and they then had thirteen years at 10 Regent Terrace from 1869, before moving to Great King Street.

In Regent Terrace Masson was visited by John Stuart Mill and Thomas Carlyle. Masson's daughter Flora wrote that Carlyle came to stay:

He complained of sleeplessness and was much troubled by the noise of the railway whistles, as the North British trains dived into the tunnel outside the Waverley station. My mother had given him a room on the drawing-room floor at the back of the house, looking out on the tall trees and Terrace gardens that slope upwards along the Calton Hill. She hoped it was a quiet room. But he heard the whistles – she could not shut out the sound. There was a room at the top of the house that had no window – only a skylight; and this was offered to Carlyle as possibly a quieter room. He went upstairs with my mother to inspect it, and seemed pleased with it. Then suddenly – down through the skylight it seemed – came the sound of a long shrill whistle, and the shriek and rattle of shunting trains. Carlyle laughed, a laugh of grim appreciation, and they went downstairs again.

Carlyle then wrote to say he had left his macintosh hanging in the hall, and asked for it to be sent in a 'brown paper parcel (unpaid) by the Caledonian Railway'.

As professor, Masson, who was said to resemble Carlyle in appearance, achieved considerable popularity. At that time students paid their fees in cash at the start of a session. When Professor Masson set off home with £300 stuffed in his pockets, some students followed him for his safety. He stopped to browse at a second-hand bookstall in the street, and purchased a volume before proceeding home.

Masson wrote extensively and readably, his chief work being a life of Milton, published over a period of twenty-one years from 1859, in six volumes: at the time this was regarded as an exhaustive biography. A residence for university women was named Masson Hall in recognition of his efforts to gain university education for women.

Two of Masson's daughters, Flora and Rosaline, were authors. They were unmarried and lived in Ann Street after their father's death.

## A Dishonest Solicitor

A solicitor who came from George Square to spend forty years at 16 Regent Terrace was William White Millar, who was President of the SSC Society 1898 – 1900. Unfortunately he continued to practice when his faculties were no longer up to it. In 1909 he pleaded guilty to embezzling £750 from a client over two and a half years – money which should have been invested on the client's wife's behalf. In mitigation it was said that his affairs were in a state of confusion, and he had suffered from some painful complaints for many years. In view of his age (a few days before his eightieth birthday) the judge gave him a 'lenient' sentence of nine months imprisonment. This was certainly less harsh than the fourteen years transportation meted out to the lawyer's clerk fifty years earlier for a similar offence. Millar presumably spent his sentence just down the road, in the Calton Jail.

## Manses

From 1871 to 1949, Greenside Church manse was at 18 Regent Terrace and was occupied by seven ministers in turn. The first was the Very Rev. Archibald Scott, DD, who became Moderator of the General Assembly of the Church of Scotland in 1896, after leaving the manse. The results of his ministry at Greenside were said to be phenomenal but there was bitterness when he left Greenside for St George's and many families, including the Session Clerk's, departed with him. Membership of Greenside at the height of his ministry reached 1,500 and raised several thousands of pounds towards the building of the Abbey Church in a new parish, formed by an amalgamation of part of Greenside parish and part of South Leith.

Among the other Ministers of Greenside Church were the Rev.John Patrick, DD, during whose ministry a Temperance Society was formed and lectures on temperance on a week night could attract a hundred people. He left Greenside to become Professor of Biblical Criticism at Edinburgh University. Another was the Rev. John Lamond, DD, whose ministry spanned the years of the First World War, during which seventy-two men of Greenside were killed in action. Dr Lamond left the established church after a personal tragedy and became a spiritualist.

London Road Church had a manse at 17 Regent Terrace from 1924 to 1946, and the house then became a temporary manse for the Canongate Kirk, occupied by the Very Rev. Ronald Selby Wright, CVO, DD, FRSE, who was also Minister of Edinburgh Castle. He has been a chaplain to the Queen for over thirty years and has been a prolific writer and broadcaster. During the Second World War, while a chaplain to the forces, he was a much loved and popular broadcaster known as the Radio Padre. In 1972-73 he was Moderator of the General Assembly of the Church of Scotland. He had the first television set in the terrace, and invited neighbours in to watch the first flight in space.

Solicitors and merchants continued to be the chief occupations among residents throughout the last quarter of the nineteenth century.

## Lord Provost and Member of Parliament

A well known merchant was James Puckering Gibson at no.33 from 1880. His family business was a high-class grocery shop in Princes Street from 1848 until it was sold to Littlewoods in 1951. Although alcohol was sold, Gibson himself was a strict teetotaller. He became Lord Provost in 1906 and three years later was elected Liberal MP for the East Division of Edinburgh and in the same year was created a baronet, dying in 1912. Sir James and Lady Gibson had no children: she stayed in the house until her death in 1941, when her nephew James Wright took over the house and lived there till 1968.

The Gibsons made extensive alterations to their house internally by replacing the stone staircase with a wooden one and by panelling all the main rooms, including over-mantels with built-in coal scuttles and a 'dumb waiter' connecting the dining-room with the basement.

Sir James joined the protest, in 1908, against the withdrawal of the cavalry from Piershill, which led to the construction of Redford Barracks. In the 1930s Lady Gibson had a Daimler, looked after by her chauffeur who lived in the mews. She also had special deliveries of foodstuffs by Gibson's vans and apparently illegally stock-piled at the outbreak of war: in 1968 a room in the basement was found to be piled to the ceiling with tinned food.

## David Livingstone's Son-in-law

At the same time as the Gibsons, Alexander Low Bruce and his family came to the terrace, to no.10, his second wife being a daughter of the missionary David Livingstone. The explorer Henry Stanley wrote later that he had 'often lodged and feasted at his hospitable house, no.10 Regent Terrace'.

Mr Bruce was Deputy Chairman of William Younger and Co. As a brewer, he persuaded Louis Pasteur to come to Edinburgh for the University's tercentenary celebrations in 1883 and to discuss Pasteur's research into fermentation problems in the French wine industry, leading to the revolutionary discovery of micro-organisms which caused disease. In his will, Bruce made a bequest to found a Chair of Public Health at Edinburgh University.

Bruce was said to have spent his money like water in the cause of Africa and especially with the object of putting an end to the slave trade. He was a trustee for the Edinburgh Medical Missionary Society in the purchase by the Society in 1877 of 39 Cowgate as the Livingstone Memorial Medical Missionary Training Institution (now used by the Scottish National Blood Transfusion Service). He and J G Bartholomew (who lived briefly with his father in Royal Terrace) founded the Royal Scottish Geogaphical Society in 1884.

On Alexander Bruce's sudden death in 1893, at the early age of fifty-four, many tributes were paid to his memory. Over 150 men gathered in Regent Terrace to follow the funeral procession in over sixty carriages to Morningside cemetery, where five or six hundred more mourners (including several ladies) were waiting.

The family did not stay in the house after 1898 but the house was owned by the family until it was given to the Church of Scotland. A plaque in the entrance hall reads: 'This house was the family home of Mr and Mrs A.L.Bruce and was given by his daughter Miss A.B.Bruce to the Foreign Mission Committee as a residence for retired missionaries. 1945.' The house was then occupied by retired missionaries for many years.

## Churchmen

Another churchman and near neighbour of Mr Bruce was John Nicholson. He was manager of the Clydesdale Bank in Edinburgh, Chairman of the

Edinburgh Chamber of Commerce, a prominent layman in the United Free Church and was closely involved with many philanthropic organisations. Just after he came to number 5 in 1885 his 27-year-old wife died in giving birth to twins. He was left to bring up four children under the age of six with the help of a housekeeper, a nurse and a housemaid. He remarried seven years later.

In May 1911, after a meeting in the Church's new offices in George Street (for which he had been largely responsible), he went home and was dictating to his wife, as he walked up and down, a report on the buildings of the church that he was to give to the approaching Assembly, when he suddenly stopped. His wife looked up and was just in time to catch him as he fell dead.

A distinguished New Testament scholar and commentator was the Very Rev. Dr Paton James Gloag, who was Moderator of the General Assembly of the Church of Scotland in 1889 shortly before retiring from his charge in Galashiels to 28 Regent Terrace, where he lived until his death in 1906. In Edinburgh he devoted himself to theological research and found recreation in the study of numismatics. His wife Elizabeth, who continued to live in their house after his death, and who died in 1914, wrote a memoir of him. She wrote that his first task after moving to Edinburgh was arranging his library and drawing up a complete catalogue, which occupied him for three months. His books were spread over the house and were arranged by subject and alphabetically by author. His quick eye would at once detect a misplaced volume.

An admirer of Dr Samuel Johnson, he formed a Johnsonian collection which was at the time unique. He instituted a club in imitation of Dr Johnson's, composed of twelve literary men, who met during the winter months in the members' houses alternately and discussed subjects of literary or scientific interest.

After retirement, Dr Gloag became interim Professor of Biblical Criticism at the University of Aberdeen for three winters, 1896 to 1899. In 1896 Aberdeen students had rebelled against the appointment to the chair of a Dr Johnston, complaining of his unfitness to teach. The case went to the House of Lords which upheld the students' complaint. Dr Gloag spoke of those three winters as an oasis in his life. After a slight stroke in 1898 he lost the power of walking and became unable to hold a pen.

He always had difficulty in recognising people, and, deep in thought, would often pass his most intimate friends. His wife said that his only extravagance was the purchase of books and that he was very careless about his appearance which was, to him, a matter of no consequence.

## Musical Chairs

Evidence of the desirability of living in Regent Terrace is shown by sixteen families who moved from one house to another within the terrace in the nineteenth century, some of them more than once. Six others moved to the terrace from Royal or Carlton Terrace and four moved out to one of those terraces. Some had tenancies which expired or had found a house to buy; others perhaps found a house more suited to their requirements. During the twentieth century, eight families have moved within the terrace (including the present Minister of State at the Scottish Office, Lord Fraser of Carmyllie) and three of them live here now, each having gone from a divided house to a whole house.

There were only thirty-three children under fifteen living in the terrace in 1891 and the number continued to decrease. Also in 1891 there were four sets of twins, aged three, five, fourteen and fifty.

## Twentieth Century

House prices had risen to about £2,500 by the end of the nineteenth century but dropped as low as £1,000 before the Second World War. Thereafter prices rose to £2,000 at the end of the war, £4,000 in the mid 1950s and approaching £400,000 today.

At the beginning of the twentieth century Ailsa Inglis was very lonely at no.29 where she came in 1902 at the age of six. She was the youngest in a solicitor's family of six and her brother and sisters were all at boarding school. She had a resident governess and she did not know any other children in the terrace.

She did go to school at Lansdowne House for one term, where, she says 'I was taught to write with my left hand as well as my right, to develop both sides of my brain'. She went there by cable-car and one day she decided to sit on the top deck where the men all sat. Going up the stairs she lost her balance but luckily was caught by a man behind her.

Miss Inglis did canteen work at the outbreak of war in 1914, and then became a VAD (member of the Voluntary Aid Detachment) in the old fever hospital in Pilton, living in the infirmary of Fettes College. 'It was not real nursing – just making beds, doing bedpans etc. We had a hockey eleven to play against the sailors who came to Rosyth.' After the end of the war, her parents moved to Drummond Place, because of the difficulty of getting servants for the big house in Regent Terrace.

## Child Labour

Albert Barnet who was born nearby in 1899 and who later lived in the mews for nearly sixty years, came up to Regent Terrace at the age of eight or ten to work before going to school. He remembers that

> there was a request from the housekeeper at number 30 for a boy to go up and clean the boots, clean the knives and forks and spoons and take in the coals. I was

approached and the wages that was offered was a little bit better than I was getting [delivering milk] so I decided to come up. It was quite good – we had an awful lot of silverware to clean. I did this for quite some time until I got a fright one morning when I met a man on the Terrace when I was going home to go to school and he pulled out a sword or stick and was going to hit me and I told my mother I wouldn't be going back again. That was my experience of upstairs and downstairs. After work I went home for something to eat, half a slice of bread or something and away to school.

## *Poetry Readings*

Another Regius Professor of Rhetoric and English Language was Sir Herbert Grierson, who lived at no.12 for more than thirty years until 1953. He was born in Lerwick: his family had been lairds in Shetland on the estate of Quendale since the mid eighteenth century. Professor Grierson was much loved, almost worshipped, by his students. He and his wife Mary Letitia Ogston had five lively daughters.

The youngest daughter, Janet, used to climb out of her bedroom window at the age of twelve or so, to join her sisters and their friends in the big gardens on summer evenings. Her older sister Alice was instrumental in organising an Armistice Day bonfire and fireworks party for the residents of all three terraces.

Janet was a pupil of Sir Donald Tovey, who sometimes escorted her home across the big garden. She wrote in 1980:

> I like to think our house still echoes with Tovey playing the piano, and my father and also W B Yeats reading poetry, and the conversation of all the exciting people that came to the house, and last but not least, G K Chesterton reciting Hilaire Belloc's *Cautionary Tales for Children* when we were still young adolescents. I can remember my mother calling up to my sister Alice at the top of the house: 'Alice, are you coming to Mr Chesterton's lecture?' and Alice's reply: 'Not bloody likely! I'm staying at home to read a detective novel!' and the long giggles that resounded from Chesterton's room on the ground-floor.

Janet married an eminent French physicist, Francois Teissier du Cros, and she was the author of *Divided Loyalties*, in which she vividly described living as a Scotswoman in occupied France during the 1939-45 War with terrible shortages of food and fuel. She also made monthly broadcasts for the BBC's Woman's Hour in the 1950s about life in Paris and the Cevennes.

Her sister Molly wrote the history of Jenners for its centenary in 1938. She prefaced it with a brief but fascinating account of life in Edinburgh during those hundred years.

## A Tea Merchant and an Engineer

Bailie William James McLaren at no.25 was a tea merchant who came here in 1915; his wife was a Macleod from Skye. He was a keen social reformer and an advocate of temperance. During the Depression of the early 1930s he instituted allotment holdings which were available free to the unemployed.

The McLarens added on a big kitchen (remembered by a neighbour as being 'as cold as charity') at the back of the house and were among the first to instal oil-fired central heating. They had a cook, a housekeeper, a tweenie and a house-boy. They had large cars, Crossleys and Morrises, and were early owners of the new Lanchesters with fluid fly wheels.

A family which spanned four generations in the terrace was that of James Bertram, who manufactured paper-making machinery. His widow and family moved to 3 Regent Terrace in 1876. Her great-grandson, another James, recalls that in the early 1930s the four children lived on the top floor with two nannies and joined their parents in the drawing-room after tea on Sundays. The children had their lessons at home with a daily governess until the age of eight. There were also a cook, housemaid, tablemaid and kitchen maid, as well as a chauffeur who lived in the mews.

The children used to accompany Nanny when she paid the household's monthly bills in Easter Road, where the shopkeepers gave the children a bar of chocolate or a small toy. Every summer the Bertrams' house was dust-sheeted and the family moved to their other home near Peebles.

## The Queen Came to Call

A royal visitor to Regent Terrace between the wars was Queen Mary who used to call on Sir Hew Dalrymple KCVO, brother of the 11th Earl of Stair. He had been Unionist MP for Wigtownshire 1915-18 before coming to no.24 in 1921. He was Captain of the Royal Company of Archers (the King's Bodyguard for Scotland), Chairman of the Board of Trustees of the National Galleries of Scotland and vice-chairman of the National Library of Scotland. He lived in this house until he died, unmarried, in 1945.

## Larger Houses

Four houses have four floors as well as a basement: these include nos 26 and 29.

The Rev. Andrew David Sloan, DD, JP, was a minister in St Andrews for forty years before retiring to Edinburgh. He came to no.29 in 1928 and was immediately elected a town councillor. He also became a director of the Zoological Society of Scotland, and a governor of the George Heriot Trust, Heriot-Watt College and Edinburgh College of Art. He had five sons and four daughters, and he used to say that their house should be warm because they had so many degrees among them.

The Rev. Cecil Taylor Thornton lived at no.26 with his second wife, two sons and a daughter, from his appointment to St Margaret's Parish Church in 1927 to his death in 1955. At one timc in the 1930s the family had six resident servants: a cook who slept in the basement, with two housemaids, a tablemaid, a nanny and a nursemaid, who all shared one large and two small bedrooms on the top floor. They had a big garage in Carlton Terrace Mews but did not have a chauffeur: if the grandmother came to stay her chauffeur came too. During the war they shared the garage with two Crimpy Crisp vans, so the children often had gifts of potato crisps.

Tradesmen's vans used to stay parked while they visited the cook, who was even taken for drives by butcher Wilson. The children enjoyed seeing the van of Crawfords, the baker, which had each wheel in the form of a rich tea biscuit. That van became horse-drawn during the war, but the McVitties Guest baker's van had never been motorised.

One year, the maids refused to cook Christmas dinner in the evening, so Mrs Thornton (who had trained as a domestic science teacher) dismissed them. She and 'Bu', who had replaced the nanny and then become a family friend, cooked the dinner. On the wages saved, Mr and Mrs Thornton went on a Hellenic cruise. The ground floor butler's pantry was then converted into a small kitchen and Mr Thornton's assistant minister lived in the basement.

There was a billiard room in the basement, with a conservatory built over it. A man called Hodge came in daily to look after the boiler and it blew up on the day that Edward VIII abdicated. The explosion destroyed the conservatory. There were other fires in the house – once when the maids carried hot ashes upstairs to their bedrooms and dropped some on the wooden stairs and once when Christmas tree candles set fire to brown paper protecting the grand piano. The family then bought an early artificial tree from Woolworths.

## Tenants

Some houses were still rented, rather than owned, by their occupiers. Number 30, which is the smallest house in the terrace, without a second floor, had a series of short-term tenants from 1910 for thirty-five years. During one tenancy, the occupiers were away for a few days, leaving behind a friend who had recently left her husband. One day the friend arrived on a neighbour's doorstep, hysterical and soaking wet. She said that the beast which had been in her husband had got into her seven-year-old son, and she had put him in the bath and knelt on him until he drowned. The nearest doctor was called and he arranged for her to be committed to a mental hospital.

Two interesting residents came briefly to no.30. One was Lady Margaret Sackville, daughter of the Earl de la Warr, who was here for two years from 1930. She was the author of many volumes of poems and of other works such as *Three Fairy Plays*. In 1922 she had published *A Masque of Edinburgh* which was performed in the Music Hall, George Street. It depicted the history of the Edinburgh people in eleven episodes, starting with the Romans and ending with a meeting between Robert Burns and Walter Scott.

Another was Francis Cadell, RSA, RSW, who was one of the four Scottish colourists. His sister was Jean Cadell, the well-known actress. In common with many other artists of the period, he was having great difficulty in making a living from sales of his paintings, which now fetch huge prices. He rented no.30 from March 1932.

Cadell was a left-handed painter. While a student, the President of the RSA told him that no left-handed artist had ever been successful. He quickly replied, 'Sir, did not Michelangelo paint with his left hand?'. The President did not respond and left the room while a fellow student asked Cadell how he had known about Michelangelo being left-handed. He said, 'I didn't know, but nor did the President'.

In Regent Terrace Cadell enjoyed the extra space, including a sunken bath and the splendid view to Arthur's Seat which can be seen in his painting *The Open Window*. Having always disliked tramcars, he wrote 'I fell down the stairs of one of our infernal tramcars and landed on the tail of my spine on one of their metal ended steps, since when I have been unable to do anything but stand up'.

In 1935 he moved to Warriston Crescent, but before leaving he held an exhibition of water-colours and drawings in his house, unfortunately attended mainly by his friends. Although in financial difficulties, he had generously presented postcard size sketches for raffles in aid of the funds of the big garden.

A neighbour remembers, 'Bunty Cadell was a most entertaining creature. He had a faithful man-servant who did everything for him. We used to be invited to wonderful dinners (long dresses and dinner jackets), all cooked and waited on by Charles'.

Stanley Cursiter described Cadell as having had

an eye that lifted to twinkle and a smile ready to expand to a quick laugh: careful in dress but seldom without a gay distinctive note – shepherd tartan trousers – a blue scarf – yellow waistcoat – or all the glory of his kilt. ... His wit was constant and brilliant.

A minister who came to no.5 in 1936 was the Rev. David Gillan, who had earlier been a chaplain in India. While a student at Glasgow University he gained several sporting awards, especially for golf. His son,

*The Open Window* by Francis Boileau Cadell showing the view from 30 Regent Terrace towards Holyrood Park. (*In a private collection. Courtesy of the Portland Gallery, London*).

Wing-Commander John Woodburn Gillan, was the first person to fly between Edinburgh and London in less than an hour, using a Hurricane fighter. He was shot down over the English Channel in August 1941 and was buried at Dunkirk.

## At War

Complying with the black-out regulations caused problems with cupolas whose glass panes could either be painted black or have panels fixed on the outside, which could be removed for part of the summer to relive the stygian gloom in the houses. At the same time, wine-cellars made admirable air-raid shelters. Some families grew vegetables and kept hens in their gardens but nothing came of the suggestion that pigs should be kept in the big garden.

## Visit of General de Gaulle

On 23 June 1942 General Charles de Gaulle, then leader of the Free French forces, officially opened the Scottish Free French House at no.28. A guard of honour, with pipe and brass bands from a Scottish Lowland regiment was inspected by the general. The house was to provide temporary shelter for men on leave before hospitality could be found for them. It would also be the centre of French culture in Scotland. The ceremony was followed by a lunch at the City Chambers and then a reception for 1,000 people at the North British Station Hotel.

A great many Free French visited the house. Some neighbours gave free bed and breakfast to French sailors from time to time.

## Non-Domestic Use of Houses

Regent Terrace was the last of the three to be occupied by commercial concerns. Not until the 1940s were there any hotels, at 6 and 7, while the residents had thought that Madame Ada's School of Dancing at 8 lowered the tone of the terrace. From 1945 to 1968 the Royal High School used nos 1, 2 and 4 as classrooms.

From the 1950s some houses were divided into flats.

One enterprising development which came to an untimely end was the restoration of the drawing-room at 23 Regent Terrace in 1969. The room was advertised in a full page of the *Scotsman*, as available for hire for functions. The furnishings were said to include a thirteen foot D-ended dining-table, eight Hepplewhite chairs, a Persian carpet, a Buhl clock and an original portrait by Sir Henry Raeburn of Mrs Alexander Fraser Tytler. The advertisement attracted thieves who managed to remove the contents of the room.

## Consular Corps

Erik Schacke, who had been Royal Danish consul since 1934, lived with his wife in no. 22 from 1946 until his death in 1969. He had come to Edinburgh at the age of twenty, ostensibly to learn the language but had fallen in love with

General Charles de Gaulle opening the new Scottish Free French House in Regent Terrace, June 1942, accompanied by the Lord Provost, Will Y Darling. (*The Scotsman Publications*).

the city. In 1957, to celebrate having lived in Edinburgh for fifty years, he bought no.11, converted it into three flats and presented it to Edinburgh Corporation to be used as grace and favour residences for worthy citizens. Unfortunately the house has never been used for the purpose for which it was given. On Mr Schacke's eightieth birthday, members of the consular corps went to his house to drink his health, as he was by then in a wheel-chair.

After the war several houses became consulates or homes for consuls. The Free French House became the French consulate, with the consul-general living on the two top floors. Later the consulate moved to the lower half of 27, leaving the consul-general to live in a whole house, as befitted his rank. The consulate is no longer in the terrace.

The United States of America acquired no.3 as a consulate, also after the war, and expanded into no.4 when the Royal High School moved out in 1968.

The Norwegian government bought no.32 as a home for its consul-general and a Greek consul lived at no.9 for a few years.

The Belgian and Danish consuls, Professor Sarolea and Mr Schacke, in procession from the City Chambers to St Giles Cathedral. (*Daily Record*).

## A Great Lady

Tertia Liebenthal, MBE, was born at number 34 and lived there all her life until she died in 1970 at the age of eighty. Her father had been a Russo-German grain merchant and had one of the first Christmas trees in Edinburgh, to be seen in his ground floor room, lit with real candles.

Miss Liebenthal inaugurated the weekly National Gallery lunch-time concerts in 1941 and collapsed and died in the Royal Scottish Academy at her 699th concert just after announcing plans for the next concert, to be given in her honour by Peter Pears and Benjamin Britten, old friends of hers. The concert went ahead, as a memorial concert.

Tertia helped to launch new performers such as Kathleen Ferrier and always insisted on at least one twentieth century work in a concert. She gave overnight hospitality to the performers and expected them to be unconventional and did not mind unmarried couples sleeping together, 'because they're artists'.

She could be very autocratic and expected neighbours to act as chauffeur. When her lodger was in bed with flu, Tertia was afraid of catching it, so she left a bottle of milk outside his door each morning and he lived on milk for a week. One evening, as she and a distinguished art historian walked home from the Cafe Royal (a favourite haunt of hers) they were alarmed to see a polar bear on the pavement and rang the doorbell of Lady Duke (a good neighbour to all and a philanthropist), who failed to find the bear – some other passer-by having removed the floor-rug from the pile of rubbish put out for the bin men.

## Post-War Residents

Norman Forrest, sculptor, never lived in his house at 16 but used it as a studio from 1949 to 1970. He did work for many pre-war passenger liners, including carving four lime-wood allegorical figures representing the four seasons for alcoves on a staircase on the liner *Queen Mary*, and designing nine bas-reliefs for the cabin-class smoking-room on the liner *Queen Elizabeth*. Among students who had studios in his house was Edward (now Sir Edward) Paolozzi who was interned in Saughton Prison at the outbreak of war. Norman Forrest used to visit Paolozzi and took him clay and modelling tools.

George Waterston, OBE, the ornithologist, lived at 21 where he established the Scottish Ornithologists' Club and the Fair Isle Trust. He purchased Fair Isle, having been captivated by it as his first sight of British land when being repatriated as a prisoner of war, and he later gave it to the National Trust for Scotland.

Other distinguished people live, and have lived, in Regent Terrace, but it is not the purpose of this book to include references to the living.

Tertia Liebenthal, a resident of Regent Terrace, who organised National Gallery concerts.

Now that the terraces are officially zoned as being for residential use, there are no hotels in Regent Terrace. The other two terraces have hotels which were either in existence before the residential zoning or have been allowed planning permission because the houses were unsuitable for family use. Apart from the US consulate at 3 and 4, the only other offices in Regent Terrace now are the Royal Society for the Protection of Birds at 17 and 21. All the rest are in private use and more than half are still whole family houses.

It is fortunate that one recommendation of the Civic Survey and Plan for Edinburgh (1949) was not implemented. Sir Patrick Abercrombie and Derek Plumstead considered that the buildings of Royal Terrace and Regent Terrace should not be listed as buildings for preservation, thereby depriving the city of valuable hotel accommodation. Instead, they recommended 'a complete re-modelling of these dwellings as hotels'.

# 4.

# ROYAL TERRACE

Royal Terrace was the first of the three terraces to have houses built in it, but it was also the last to be completed, taking nearly fifty years from start to finish. Possibly there was not enough demand for such large houses once the New Town had been populated.

The first house to be built was at the east end (now no.40) and this is the only one to be shown on the Lothian map of 1825. An anonymous diarist observed in October 1823 that 'The Royal Terrace, notwithstanding its elevated and commanding position, is feuing out but slowly and as yet only three of its houses are inhabited'. By June 1825 he could report 'The Royal Terrace which, for a long time past, consisted of seven houses not the half inhabited, from the digging going on is about to receive some additions'. A year later again he wrote 'The Royal Terrace, after standing long at seven houses is now increased to twelve'. Not all of them were yet occupied.

The terrace was gradually built in three blocks of houses with two gaps left in the middle and a space at the west end for the completion of Playfair's design. The houses were numbered 4 to 14 inclusive, 18 to 25 inclusive and 30 to 35 inclusive. From the middle 1830s for about twenty years these gap sites remained unfilled. The second gap was filled in 1854-1859. In 1859 nos 1 to 3 were occupied.

From 1860 houses began to be occupied in the first gap which was large enough for eight houses although only three numbers (15 to 17) were available. To deal with the lack of numbers, the existing numbers 18 to 35 were renumbered 23 to 40 in 1860. These new numbers are used throughout this book, even where referring to pre-1860 houses.

## *First Residents*

The first person to live in Royal Terrace was Thomas Dallas, a wine and spirit merchant of Physic Gardens, who came to no.40 for eleven years from

1822. He was followed a year later by Neil Ryrie, a brewer from St Anne's brewery in Abbeyhill, who came from the Grassmarket to no.39.

The houses were slow to be occupied with, at first, only one new household each year. By 1830 they included two Robert Halls, a merchant and WS, probably father and son, at no.36 and a family of four solicitors called Ellis at no.4: they had their offices in their house, having previously been in Albany Street. William Ellis became President of the SSC Society 1838-40. John Mackinlay of Newlandburn in Midlothian was another spirit dealer who came here. He and his brother David and two sisters all lived unmarried at no.30, the last sister remaining until 1893. James Mackinlay, who lived at no.40 for twenty years towards the end of the century was probably a relative.

Another firm of solicitors also worked in their home. Gordon, Stewart and Cheyne WS had their offices first at 26 and then at 5, the successive homes for twenty years of Joseph Gordon from 1836, while his partner Henry Cheyne came to live next door at no.6 with his seven children and five resident servants.

Some houses were used even before they were completed. For instance, no.35 was built for Admiral Duncan, who never lived there. It was occupied for five years from 1836 by Alexander Hunter, WS, and then used as a boarding house by a Mrs Sheriff, still in an unfinished condition.

Solicitors and merchants continued to arrive here, and, on the whole, to stay here, often through two generations. It was quite usual for unmarried sons and daughters to continue to live with their parents, and to stay on together after their parents' deaths. Andrew Tawse, WS, came to no.10 in 1831 from York Place with his wife and five children. Five years later and with one more child they moved next door to no.11 . The eldest son John, another WS, later became head of the household with three sisters and a brother, all unmarried and all living there until their deaths, the last sister dying in 1908.

## Greenside Church

A church was needed to serve the people living on the east side of Calton Hill. Until a site was found some residents met for worship in a hall in Waterloo Place from 1832. Four years later, the Presbytery of Edinburgh agreed to form a new parish of Greenside out of part of St Cuthbert's parish, and chose a site at the western end of Royal Terrace.

The architect was James Gillespie Graham. Originally a joiner from Dunblane, he rose to become a distinguished architect. On marriage to an heiress, he added her surname of Graham to his own of Gillespie. The church was completed in 1839, although the tower was not built until 1851. Galleries were added in 1846 but removed in 1885.

Greenside Church, at the west end of Royal Terrace.

The church was originally heated by coal-fired stoves which caused so much smoke that the church had to be closed annually for a week for the walls to be cleaned. A form of central heating with heat rising through cast-iron grids in the floor was installed in 1879. The first organ was installed in 1890 and replaced in 1933 with the present organ.

The first minister of Greenside Church was the Rev.William Glover, DD, who remained in post until his death in 1871, by which time the congregation had grown to 700 members, despite the Disruption of 1843. Divinity students were attracted to the church by Dr Glover, who took a particular interest in them.

After Dr Glover's death the church acquired a manse at 18 Regent Terrace, previously occupied by Alexander Goodsir, a banker. The house continued in use as a manse until 1949, after which the parish had to economise because of the expense of considerable structural repairs to the church. Ministers who lived in the Regent Terrace manse have been described in Chapter 3.

Robert Louis Stevenson, whose grandparents, father and uncles had lived in a large house in nearby Baxter's Place, referred to Greenside Church as 'the church on the hill'. That is the title of a small book by Neil Taverner giving the history of the church and its activities.

## Members of Parliament

A house which went through various family relationships was no.13 where James and Walter Marshall, jewellers and goldsmiths of 41 George Street, lived from 1839 with two unmarried sisters and James's son Francis. In 1862 James's daughter married Major Walter Ferrier Hamilton of Cairnhill, Craigie and they started their married life in this house. Hamilton's father, of the same name, had been a Royal Navy Lieutenant who had commanded the party of sailors who dragged the cannon up the Heights of Abraham, before the capture of Quebec in 1759.

Hamilton was MP for Linlithgowshire while living here: his brother-in-law Andrew Gillon took over the house in 1875 till his death in 1888, after which Gillon's wife and children stayed on till 1922. But the Gillons apparently let the house for six years from 1894 to Sheriff (later Sir) David Brand who needed to live in Edinburgh while he was chairman of the Royal Commission on the Highlands and Islands, having earlier been Chairman of the Crofters' Commission.

When Andrew Gillon came here his first wife Jane (Walter Hamilton's sister) was dead, as was his second wife. Andrew Gillon's father, William Downe Gillon of Wallhouse, had been another MP (for Falkirk burghs) who lived in the terrace at no.25 until his death in 1846. One of Andrew Gillon's sons by his third wife, Stair Agnew Gillon, lived at 14 Carlton Terrace after his marriage in 1919. Members of one family had ninety years in the two terraces, in three different houses.

## Boarding Schools

Apart from solicitors' offices, another non-domestic use for these houses was as boarding schools. By 1841 there were two of these: one at no.39 was run by a 65-year-old woman, Mrs Isabella Bisset and her five adult daughters, with eight girls aged fifteen to nineteen. The other, at no.12, was headed by Mrs Margaret Campbell who had six resident female servants to help in looking after sixteen children aged from five to twenty and who came from five families, so most had brothers or sisters for company. Mrs Campbell probably had teachers coming in daily.

It is likely that both of those houses took in children whose fathers were serving overseas. Officers of the Honourable East India Company (HEICS) began to find homes in Royal Terrace, some having retired young, while others left their families here on returning to India. The first such officer was David Marshall who came to no.10 with his wife and baby daughter, the first of their four children, in 1840. He had been a Captain in the East India Company Maritime Service. He was twenty years older than his wife, who survived him: she lived in this house for over fifty years.

In the early 1860s two houses were used as commercial boarding houses. One was at no.9 where Mrs William Thomson, a factor's widow, took in eleven boarders aged from sixty-seven down to fifteen. All were unmarried and none had an occupation, most being described in the census as 'fund holder' or of independent means.

The other, at no.26, was a school from 1860 for over twenty years. The 1861 census showed the householder to be Miss Elizabeth Weir, school-mistress, with three resident governesses including Miss Marie du Plessis and seventeen girl pupils aged thirteen to eighteen, and also one 22-year-old female boarder and three servants. Ten years later, Miss du Plessis, now aged forty-nine, had taken charge and had one partner. They were aided by two female teachers, one being Miss du Plessis' sister. There were then nineteen girl scholars, aged fourteen to seventeen and four servants of whom one had been cook ten years earlier.

By 1881 the teaching staff had all changed and were headed by Miss Dora Remmers who had three governesses, one each for music (her sister), English and French. Only two girls were resident, so others probably came in daily for their lessons. There were fifty young people aged sixteen to nineteen in the terrace at that time, so Miss Remmers should have had no difficulty in finding pupils.

## Moving from House to House

While some families enjoyed a long occupancy of one house, others moved from house to house. Mrs Catherine Miller of Earnock in Lanarkshire, had one year in no.37, followed by ten years at no.26 (which changed to that number while she lived there) and then, in 1860 she took advantage of a new house having been built at 17 to return to the terrace after an absence of five years.

## Census Returns

Not surprisingly, the large houses in Royal Terrace attracted large families. At the 1841 census there were sixty-seven children aged fifteen or under and also sixteen aged sixteen to twenty. By 1871 these numbers had increased to eighty and sixty respectively.

Of all the nineteenth century censuses, that of 1851 showed the highest density of population in the terrace, with an average of ten people living in each house. A cluster of three houses, nos 35 to 37, each had twenty-two residents. The families were those of, first, Alexander Cowan (of whom more presently) who had thirteen family members, three visitors, a governess and five domestic servants. Second, at no.36 was Alan Dun-lop, described as a fund holder (India Company) with ten family members, ten of his own servants and two who had come with visiting relatives. Third, at no.37, having a few years earlier had one year at 38, was Robert Stewart, a landed proprietor of Carfin, Lanarkshire who, with his wife, had eleven children at home, two visitors and six servants (two being attached to the nursery).

Throughout the century the houses each had an average of four resident domestic servants, almost all female. At each census there were five or six male servants, usually butlers or footmen. In 1871 two houses each had a page: a fourteen-year-old at no.1(for John Colquhoun, retired army officer) and a twelve-year-old at no.13 for Major Walter Hamilton, former MP.

## A Patriarch

No family had a firmer footing in the terraces than the Cowans. Duncan Cowan was the first to arrive and was at 1 Carlton Terrace from 1835 to 1848, and he died there at the age of seventy-seven. Sir Walter Scott referred to him as 'honest Duncan, the paper-manufacturer'. One of his great interests while living there was planning and laying out the gardens on Calton Hill. Duncan had nine children, one of whom, Janet, later lived in Royal Terrace.

Duncan's brother Alexander came to 35 Royal Terrace in 1845, aged seventy, and lived there until his death in 1859. Alexander Cowan was the thirteenth of fourteen children and was the founder of Alexander Cowan and Sons, papermakers, Penicuik. He came to Royal Terrace from Moray House in the Canongate, where he had lived as a tenant since 1828. He was twice married and had twenty children, eleven by his first wife Elizabeth Hall and nine by his second Helen Brodie, whose sister Janet married Duncan Cowan – so the two brothers married two sisters. Later Duncan's daughter Charlotte married Alexander's son James. The pattern was repeated in the next generation, when Alexander's daughter and son, Helen and Charles, married Allan and Catherine Menzies, brother and sister.

Alexander's first wife, Elizabeth, established a school for children of working people. A peeress, the wife of a Cabinet Minister, told her it was wise and proper to teach children to read, but on no account to write, for they would be sure to use their knowledge for the purposes of forgery.

The paper mills and the Cowans' mansion house at Penicuik had been a prison for 6,000 French prisoners of war from 1810 to 1814. In 1820 Alexander bought his buildings back from the government and the cast-iron columns which carried double tiers of prisoners' hammocks could still be seen in 1915. He put up a memorial to the 309 prisoners who died there and it was visited in 1831 by the exiled young Duke of Bordeaux (heir to the French throne), resident at Holyrood.

*Alexander Cowan and his Family* by Kenneth Macleay, 1839. From left – Charles, MP, Helen (Mrs Menzies), Elizabeth (Mrs Thompson), Alexander, Duncan, Lucy (Mrs Constable), Sir John, James, MP, and Marjorie (Mrs Simpson). The family is pictured at Moray House. (*In a private Scottish Collection*).

Alexander was once stirred with pity for residents of the Canongate whose windows were broken or stuffed with paper and rags. He gave his glazier orders to glaze all broken windows from Castlehill to Holyrood. His liberality was unbounded – it is said that he gave away half of his income in works of love and kindness, but he hated public acknowledgement or even knowledge of his gifts.

Alexander was an eminently domestic man, living much in the heart of his family, beginning the day by reading and studying with his daughters from 6 to 8 am, coming home punctually every afternoon at three o'clock and calling to them 'I'll give you two and a half minutes to get ready' before going for a walk with them. He held a great family gathering every Christmas Eve round the Christmas tree, where friends and relatives met who had no other chance of meeting during the year; this custom was continued by his son James in later years in the same house at 35 Royal Terrace. On the twenty-fifth anniversary of Alexander's second marriage, sixty-three descendants signed a congratulatory address and presented a china tea-set, designed and made for the occasion. On his tombstone in Grange cemetery is the information that he left sixty-one descendants. Twenty years later his son Charles claimed that there were by then 104 surviving descendants of Alexander.

Alexander's son James (later Sir James) lived briefly at no.24 and then at 38 Royal Terrace from 1853 for ten years, before taking over his parents' house until his death in 1895. He was elected to the Town Council in 1848 but retired after one year, being too much engaged with his business of paper-manufacturing. He was elected again in 1872, as an opponent of the Town Council's scheme to utilise St Mary's Loch to increase the water supply to the city. The bill for that purpose was thrown out and he was then Lord Provost for two years before being elected MP for Edinburgh in 1874 for the 'Aggregate Liberal Committee'. He resigned from Parliament in 1882.

James had a reckless temperament. One warm day, he stripped and jumped into a quarry full of water but then found he could not climb out. He was so long in the water that he was seriously ill in consequence.

After James had died, one of Alexander's grandsons Robert Charles Menzies, SSC, came to live at no. 35, which thus housed three generations over more than sixty years. Robert was one of nine children of Helen Cowan and Prof. Allan Menzies, WS.

Meanwhile Alexander's son Charles lived two doors from his father at no.37 for a few years from 1855. He was elected MP for the City of Edinburgh in 1847, having stood against Lord Macaulay, but the election was declared void because he had been party to a government contract. He was elected again a few months later without opposition, and remained as MP until 1859.

Charles must have had a keen sense of humour, for, in 1835, he set out to meet and honestly outwit the regulations of the Post Office. These required that every letter should be written on a single sheet of not more than one ounce in weight. Paper was made at Valleyfield Mills four feet by three feet six inches, weighing under one ounce, to the great annoyance of the Post Office who, judging by apparent bulk, charged treble postage and were frequently compelled to refund the overcharge.

Charles had been present at Queen Victoria's coronation in Westminster Abbey in 1837 and, determined that she should hear his voice, he led with a ringing shout *God Save the Queen*. He published his reminiscences privately in 1878 and presented a copy to Gladstone.

Duncan Cowan's daughter Janet and her husband Lt.Gen. Charles Wahab of the Madras Army rented her cousin Charles's house at 37 Royal Terrace from 1860 until Charles gave it up in 1864. They then moved next door to what had been James's house at no. 38. They had ten children of whom one son, Charles, went on an expedition with Archibald Ross Colquhoun, FRGS, to explore the then unknown districts of China between Hong Kong and Burma. The severe march of 1,800 miles in a malarious country proved fatal and Charles Wahab died on the way home and was buried in the Red Sea. Janet Wahab outlived her husband by more than twenty years, and their daughter Charlotte continued to live at no.38 into the next century.

Thomas Constable, printer, came to live at no. 34 in 1855, having married Alexander Cowan's daughter Lucy in 1837, so she lived next door to her father for four years. Alexander had paid for the continuing education in Germany of Thomas (his future son-in-law) and his brother when their father Archibald Constable (head of the publishing and book-selling firm in Edinburgh) became bankrupt and said the debt should be repaid 'by our children's children'. Thomas did not manage to restore his father's publishing house to its former reputation because of competition from London. He wrote: 'the debt remains uncancelled and the generous donor crowned the obligation ten years later by the gift of a daughter as my wife, so that their children's children owe each other naught but love'. Thomas and Lucy had nine children who no doubt ran in and out of Alexander's house. Thomas was said to have a sweet and genial nature and a fund of genuine Scottish humour.

Another terrace marriage in the Cowan family was that of Janet, one of Alexander's daughters. She married a neighbour Robert Boog Watson, LLD, one of the twelve children of the Rev. Dr Charles Watson who had lived for a few years at 19 Royal Terrace and had moved to 13 Carlton Terrace in 1847. Robert was a chaplain to the forces in the Crimea and during the Indian Mutiny and was a noted conchologist and geologist. One of Robert's and Janet's daughters was Helen Bannerman who was the

Cover of *The Story of Little Black Sambo* by Helen Bannerman, who was born in Royal Terrace. (*Courtesy of Reinhardt Books and Ragged Bears*).

author of *The Story of Little Black Sambo* and other popular childrens' books. Helen was born at her great-grandfather's house, 35 Royal Terrace, and lived there for her first two years.

All these large families of Cowans had many domestic servants to serve their households. No.35 always had five or six resident servants. Alexander's son Charles Cowan wrote:

> We generally were able to select from the families of our work people young girls who, after being trained, became admirable servants. We have one such female domestic at present who has been 42 years in this house. Another, though not trained here, has been in the family 22 years. There must have been probably not fewer than 150 domestic female servants in all in my house during the 53 years of my married and widowed life.

## *Links with Robert Louis Stevenson*

Two uncles of Robert Louis Stevenson lived in the terraces. Both were civil engineers. The older one, Alan, had four years at 25 Regent Terrace from 1848. He designed and built ten lighthouses, including Skerryvore, built on a rock fourteen miles from the nearest land, the Isle of Tiree. His brother David was a recognised authority on the improvement of rivers and construction of harbours and docks. He had fifteen years at 25 Royal Terrace from 1855, having succeeded Alan as engineer to the Northern Lighthouse Board. He designed and executed twenty-eight beacons and thirty lighthouses, some being in India, Newfoundland, New Zealand and Japan. He took a leading part in introducing paraffin for lighthouse illumination.

Alan and David and their brother Thomas (RLS's father) gave part of their family garden in Baxter Place in 1864 to be used for a Church of Scotland chapel for the poor of Greenside parish.

Perhaps it was Robert Louis Stevenson's familiarity with his uncles' houses that led to his hero in *The Misadventures of John Nicholson* having a male friend in Regent Terrace and a young lady friend in Royal Terrace.

## *Wine Merchants and Others*

Royal Terrace was known as Whisky Row, probably – it was said – because merchants could look out of their north-facing windows and see their ships arriving at Leith. Another possible explanation is that an increasing number of wine merchants came to live here and most of them stayed for many years.

During the 1860s, seven wine merchants lived in the terrace. John Crabbie, best known for his firm's ginger wine, was the son of an upholsterer who lived in the Canongate with his ten children. Two other sons went to America and fought in the Civil war; John came to no.22 in 1861 and remained there till his death thirty years later.

James Cree covered the same span of years at no.34 and his son William, also a wine merchant, then briefly lived in Carlton Terrace. Thomas Elder, son of a farmer (and quite likely of the same family as Thomas Elder, wine merchant, who was three times Lord Provost in the 1790s) was at no.40 from 1856 until his death in 1869. James and Alexander Hutchison arrived at no.28 in 1863: a nephew Thomas Hutchison, also a wine merchant, lived there until 1920. The shortest stay by a wine merchant at that time was that of John Shiels, who spent ten years at no.8 with his wife and seven children.

Most merchants who lived here had their businesses in Leith or in or near the Old Town. Two exceptions were William Renton and Alexander Gray. William Renton, at no.20 from 1865, was a silk mercer at 12 – 14 Princes Street, where the shop had been established in 1816 by his father.

His letter-heads advertised home and foreign outfits, marriage trousseaux and Paris modes.

Alexander Gray was an ironmonger, employing forty-six men and twenty-two boy apprentices when he came to no.4 in 1871. He had eight children. His father, James Gray, had come to Edinburgh to seek his fortune with all his belongings wrapped in a turkey red handkerchief: he had opened his own shop in Leith Wynd in 1818. As he was not a freeman nor a burgess of the city he incurred the jealousy of members of the Incorporated Trades. However, the burgh boundary ran through his shop and he could enter from outside the line but he could not risk going outside to put up his shutters which he made to fasten from the inside. Eight years later his business was established in York Lane and he did some work for the Palace of Holyroodhouse. In 1836 his son Alexander joined the business. In the middle of the century the firm moved to George Street and obtained a royal warrant as 'stove and grate-makers in ordinary to Her Majesty'. In 1888, Alexander Gray retired, but the business is still in the same premises today.

In an allied occupation was John Richard, a type-founder of Miller and Company, at no.23. As a young man he had lived with his parents and siblings at 24 Regent Terrace; his father had employed 294 men and boys in 1851, by which time John was a partner. By the time that he came to Royal Terrace in 1868 he had a large family, eventually increasing to nine children. For a few years they would have been able to run through the big garden to visit their grandparents, who then moved to George Square.

## Long Occupancies

Many other families had long occupancies of houses here. Major John Colquhoun was the first occupier of no.1 in 1859, with his wife and eight children and six resident servants. He had retired from the 4th Dragoon Guards and was a keen sportsman and a sporting writer, the author of *The Moor and the Loch* and other books. After his death the house passed to his son Sir Alan Colquhoun, KCB, 13th Baronet of Colquhoun and Luss and chief of the clan, who lived here until his death in 1910.

Covering roughly the same dates was the family of Adam Crawford of the East India Company Maritime Service, who came to no.19 in 1861 as the first occupant. A son and an unmarried daughter kept the house until 1916.

## Clergy

While minister of Lady Yester's Church in Infirmary Street, the Very Rev. Dr William H Gray had his home first at 26 Royal Terrace from 1855 (after his marriage to Mary, daughter of Robert Mitchell of 8 Regent Terrace) and then at 5 Regent Terrace. He went briefly to 3 Carlton Terrace in 1880 in which year he became minister of Liberton Church, but kept his house for his retirement, thus enjoying over fifty years in the three terraces. While at Liberton he was Moderator of the General Asssembly of the Church of Scotland.

Academics and clergy were either not drawn to, or could seldom afford to live in Royal Terrace. One of the first academics was the Rev.Prof. William Stevenson who was thankful to be appointed to the chair of Ecclesiastical History in 1861. He had had eighteen years of strained relationships with his assistant minister at South Leith Church, following the rebuilding of the church and the consequent loss in seat rents. His sermons were admired as examples of meticulous preparation and he amassed an immense library, for which his house at no.37 must have been more suitable than his manse in Hermitage Place, Leith. He was said to be tall, thin, and of a retiring disposition, with a somewhat forbidding manner.

Shortly before Professor Stevenson's death, another minister came to the terrace. This was the Rev. William Robertson, DD, Minister of New Greyfriars from 1843 for nearly forty years, who died soon after retiring to no.39. His widow continued to live there for another ten years. Dr Robertson was described as 'a man of rare spiritual gifts and consecration'. He devoted himself to developing Home Mission work in the Grassmarket on lines which have since been widely followed. The Vennel Ragged School, established by him in 1846, was the first of its kind in Edinburgh. The William Robertson Memorial Church in the Grassmarket was erected to his memory. He took a deep interest in the work of the Waldensian Club (a religious sect) and, along with Drs Guthrie and Andrew Thomson, raised £12,000 on its behalf. He had five sons and one daughter but none lived in the terrace.

## Astronomers-Royal for Scotland

The next academic was a colourful figure, Charles Piazzi Smyth, who came from Hillside Crescent to no. 15 in 1870 to live in his official residence as Astronomer-Royal for Scotland. He was simultaneously Professor of Astronomy. He had been born in Naples, the second son of Admiral William Henry Smyth, and was named after his godfather, the Italian astronomer Guiseppe Piazzi of Palermo.

Piazzi Smyth's marriage to Jessie Duncan in 1855 was childless. She was his constant companion on his travels. On their honeymoon they went on a scientific expedition to Tenerife where he founded the major observatory on Mount Teide, which is now operated by the Royal Observatory in Edinburgh.

Professor Piazzi Smyth was the first man to photograph the inside of the Pyramids. He later resigned as a Fellow of the Royal Society when the

Professor Charles Piazzi Smyth, Astronomer Royal for Scotland.
(*Courtesy of the Royal Observatory*).

society refused to publish his papers on 'pyramidology', about his belief that the dimensions of the Great Pyramid contained mathematical and physical laws hidden in mystical combinations.

He had time for research and practical activities because, although he was Professor of Astronomy, his subject was not required for graduation in any degree. Consequently, he said, 'there are generally no students at all for so untoward, despised and poverty-stricken a subject'. From the top floor of his house in Royal Terrace he had a wonderful vantage point from which he made important studies of the Aurora Borealis and night luminous clouds.

Piazzi Smyth was described by Professor H A Bruck, one of his twentieth century successors, as 'one of the most colourful personalities in the scientific world of the nineteenth century'.

He was succeeded in 1889 by Dr Ralph Copeland, who was the third Astronomer-Royal for Scotland and the fourth Regius Professor of Astronomy. As a young man Copeland had worked for five years in Victoria, Australia, partly on a sheep run and partly on gold-digging. On his return he married his first cousin Susannah Milner, who died seven years later in 1866. He then served on the second German Arctic expedition in 1869-70 before marrying Theodora, daughter of the orientalist Professor Benfey of Göttingen; they had three daughters and one son. Before coming to Edinburgh, Copeland was Director of Astronomy to the Earl of Crawford and Balcarres at his private observatory at Dunecht, near Aberdeen.

Under Copeland, a new Royal Observatory was opened in 1895 on Blackford Hill, to replace the virtually obsolete one on Calton Hill. A BSc degree in astronomy was at last instituted at the University of Edinburgh.

## A Distinguished Cartographer

John Bartholomew, FRGS, the son of the founder of the firm of that name, was a map engraver who lived at no.32 for the last six years of his life. Towards the end of the 1870s he had introduced contour layer colouring to maps: the colours had to be applied one at a time, in separate printings and of course had to be extremely precise. He had been responsible for the famous map of Treasure Island which he had engraved under instructions from Robert Louis Stevenson. The copper plate is still in the firm's archives. He also drew on stone the official artist's impression of the proposed Forth Railway Bridge – a design which was never used. His major achievement was the production of the Reduced Ordnance series of maps, showing England and Scotland in the two scales of four and two miles to the inch.

In 1887, the year of Queen Victoria's golden jubilee, he wrote to his son John George that over forty bonfires could be seen from Calton Hill, with a splendid blaze on Arthur's Seat. That son and a grandson, yet another John, were cartographers to King George V.

Three generations of the Bartholomew family: John (1831-93), John (1890-1962) and John George (1860-1920).

In the month in which he died, in 1893, his wife used the services of a coach hirer, I and R Leggat of Regent Terrace Lane, on most days. Some journeys were 'to school' for one shilling – presumably for his three teenage daughters by his second wife, his other eight children being adult by then. Others were for an hour's airing (three shillings), to the railway station or to Bartholomew's offices. For twenty-seven separate journeys the bill came to £1.11.0.

John Bartholomew's widow offered the house for sale in 1906 by public roup (auction) with an upset (reserve) price of £2,200. The house was advertised as having four public rooms, six bedrooms, a handsome entrance hall and inner lobby, a butler's pantry, kitchen, excellent lavatory and sanitary equipment (the drainage having been recently renewed), ample servants' accommodation and other conveniences. There was hot water throughout the house, speaking tubes and other appliances.

This was a bad time for selling a house in Royal Terrace as six were simultaneously on the market, with a further four a few months later. That is to say, one quarter of the terrace was for sale. Advertised prices were reduced several times. No.6 was reduced from £2,200 to £1,000 over a two year period. The Bartholomew house was rented to a succession of tenants and was eventually sold in 1923 for £1,200.

In 1907, when the house was unoccupied, a passing policeman noticed a broken window pane. On investigation, he found that a number of gas brackets had been torn from their sockets. He discovered the culprits hiding in a press at the top of the house. One, aged nineteen and with four previous convictions, was sent to prison for forty days and the other, aged seventeen with one previous conviction, for fourteen days.

## Spreading Families

Many families had father and son, or brothers, in different houses in the terraces. One family spread itself over six houses. Two brothers, Adam Dawson and John Gillon Dawson lived at 36 and 24 from the middle 1880s. They were wine merchants trading at Assembly Street and Mitchell Street.

Adam lived at 36 for thirty years. His elder son Alexander Bashall Dawson, CA, moved from there to no.33 in about 1910. Adam's younger son Percy had already moved to no.7.

J G Dawson remained at 24 until the late 1920s. Of his five children, two sons acquired homes in the terraces: John Douglas Dawson at 23 Regent Terrace and Eric F Dawson at 12 Carlton Terrace. Number 24 became a Royal High School boarding-house from 1927, with D H M Dawson as house master.

Another two-generation family was that of the Keppie Patersons. John (of Hugh Paterson, plumbers, in Elm Row) had over forty years at no.30

Street, on Wednesday, 29th January 1908, at 2.15 o'clock Afternoon, unless previously disposed of by private bargain, that SUPERIOR WEST END DWELLING HOUSE, consisting of Diningroom, Drawingroom, Library, Bed and Dressing Rooms on Drawingroom Flat, 3 Bedrooms, Bathroom, &c., on Third Flat, Two Attic Bedrooms, with Bathroom, &c., Lavatory, &c., on Ground Floor, Good Kitchen Accommodation in Area, also Scullery, Laundry, with White Ware Tubs, and 2 Servants' Rooms, with Cupboards and Cellarage. There is good Back Green Accommodation.

Rent. £148. Feu-duty, £18. 4s.

Apply to MACKENZIE, INNES, & LOGAN, W.S., 23 Queen Street, who have the Titles and Articles of Roup, and who will give cards of admission.

## ROYAL TERRACE, No. 6.

To be Exposed for SALE by Public Roup. within Dowell's Rooms, 18 George Street, on Wednesday, 22d January 1908, at 2 o'clock (if not previously Sold Privately), this SELF-CONTAINED DWELLINGHOUSE, containing Three Public Rooms, Four Bedrooms with Two Dressingrooms, Bathroom and Lavatories, Kitchen, Pantries, Washhouse and Larders, suitable Servants' Accommodation, Cellarage, and other Conveniences. Proprietor has right to enjoy the very attractive Private Terrace, Garden behind. Feu-duty, £18, 16s. Entry Taxed.

VERY LOW UPSET PRICE,
£1400
(to include Grates, Fenders, Fire-Irons, Gas Fittings, and Blinds in House.)

Seen daily by Card only from 10 to 4. Apply to GILLESPIE & PATERSON, W.S., 31 Melville Street

## ROYAL TERRACE, No. 32.

For SALE by Public Roup, at Dowell's, Wednesday, 29th January, at 2.30.

LARGE DWELLING-HOUSE of Three Floors and Basement Floor, well lighted, and perfectly dry. Handsome Entrance Hall; Drainage Equipment recently renewed; good Back Green and Garden, with access to the Private Grounds; Hot Water throughout. Speaking Tubes, &c.

Feu-duty, £18, 14s. Upset Price, £1500.

WISHART & SANDERSON, W.S. 15 York Place, Edinburgh.

## ROYAL TERRACE (33), Edinburgh—

LARGE DWELLING-HOUSE of Five Storeys, with Garden, for Sale, in Dowell's Rooms, on Wednesday, 8th January 1908, at 2.30 P.M., unless previously Sold by Private Bargain. Entry on payment or at Whitsunday. Feu-duty, £17, 12s. Entries Taxed. Fee full. REDUCED UPSET, £1650.

For further particulars apply to WALLACE & BEGG, W.S., 14 Frederick Street.

## ROYAL TERRACE, 21.—For SALE by Private

Bargain. DWELLING-HOUSE, No. 21 ROYAL TERRACE, containing 3 Public Rooms, 8 Bedrooms, Dressingroom, 3 Bathrooms, 2 Servants' Bedrooms, Laundry, &c.; this is one of the Largest Houses in the Terrace, and is in the best condition as to decoration and sanitation. Feu-duty, £18, 10s. Apply to J. & J. Milligan, W.S., 15 York Place.

## RUTLAND SQUARE, No. 14.—To be SOLD by

Public Roup, within Dowell's Rooms, No. 18 George Street, Edinburgh, on Wednesday, 15th January 1908, at 2 o'clock Afternoon, this Excellent and Commodious DWELLING-HOUSE, containing Diningroom, Morning Room, Draw-

Royal Terrace house advertisements in 1907.

from 1897. He just overlapped with his son Arthur who lived for over thirty years at no.14 and was chairman of the gardens committee for twenty-five of those years. John's father, George Keppie Paterson, was associated with the Edinburgh Medical Missionary Society in the Cowgate for over fifty years as its director, treasurer, vice-president and director of its choir.

## President of the Royal Scottish Academy

George (later Sir George) Reid came to no.22 in 1892, after six years at 17 Carlton Terrace. He had given up landscape work for what later Victorians sometimes called 'the sin of commission' that is, commissioned portraits. As a portrait painter, he was exclusively a painter of men and never of women.

On becoming President of the RSA in 1891 (a position he held for eleven years), he discovered the Academy's affairs to be in a sorry state. He surrendered his right to the president's honorarium, cancelled fees paid for attendance at council meetings and reduced the number of pictures hung, pointing out that 'the hangers showed the most wonderful ingenuity. You would not have seen a foot of bare wall from the floor up to the ceiling and under the archways down to the floor'. This long-established practice had led to an exhibitor in 1844 regretting that as his painting 'had been exalted to grace the ceiling no one is likely to trouble me'.

## Schools Inspectorate

John Kerr, who had lived at 13 Regent Terrace for six years and retired to 15 Royal Terrace in 1900, was Senior Chief Inspector of Schools and Training Colleges in Scotland. During his forty-seven years as an inspector, he examined the majority of the secondary schools in Scotland and gave evidence before almost all important Education Commissions. His final verdict on Scottish education, after his retirement, was that 'the greatest single contribution to practical education has been the demonstration of the nursery school [for the under 5s] as the requirement of every child of civilisation'. He seems to have been a prophet before his time.

## End of the Nineteenth Century

At the time of the 1891 census the number of residents in the terrace was 289, reduced from the peak of 366 in 1871. There were fewer children under sixteen: only twenty-nine in 1891 compared with eighty in 1871. The days of very large families were nearly over. Similarly, the number of resident domestic servants had been reduced from 152 to 126.

The number of householders of independent means had declined over the years from ten in 1841 to six in 1891. One, Mrs Henrietta Pritchard, the widow of a veterinary surgeon of the Madras army, had seven sons and one daughter living with her at no.7. Householders' occupations in 1891 covered a wide range. They included confectioner (William Steedman at no.3), hop and porter agent (Charles Morrison at no.25 with a brother William who was a wine merchant at no.29), a publisher (Thomson Boyd of Oliver and Boyd at no.14) and two printers (William Gibb, chairman of Morrison and Gibb, at no.21 and James Tod of Mould and Tod, engravers of lithographs with sixty-nine employees in St James Square, at no.16), a steamship owner (Hugh Black at no.8) and a brewer (Thomas Drybrough at no.31, whose father Andrew had earlier lived at 14 Regent Terrace).

## Men of the Law

After its early days, Royal Terrace did not attract solicitors until Charles Ritchie SSC came to no.37 and J Campbell Irons, SSC and some of his five sons (two being solicitors) came to no.10 for the last seven years of the nineteenth century. J C Irons published several manuals which became standard works on police law, licensing law and other subjects. He also wrote a two volume work on Leith and its antiquities.

No practicising advocates lived in any of the three terraces until after the 1939-1945 War, with the one exception of Thomas Thomson at 16 Regent Terrace from 1842. The reason was probably that advocates were expected to live within an even shorter distance from the Court of Session, so that their papers could be easily delivered to their homes.

## Chief Constable

A different side of the law was represented by Roderick Ross, Chief Constable of Edinburgh from 1900 to 1935. He came to no.12 in 1921 for one year only before moving to no.34 for ten years. A Scot, originally from Sutherland, he had earlier been Chief Constable for Ramsgate and for Bradford. He had four sons (two of whom also became Chief Constables, of Argyll and of Sutherland) and five daughters. Roderick Ross bore a remarkable resemblance to King George V.

Ross was responsible for the installation of the police box system in the city, and under his direction automatic street signals and wireless equipment were introduced; the force was mechanised and a regular mounted section established. During the General Strike of 1926 he mobilised a large force of special constables and handled demonstrations with tact and firmness. He took a keen interest in social welfare and particularly in the Edinburgh Police-Aided Scheme for Providing Boots and Clothing for Poor Children.

In 1933 he moved to 28 Regent Terrace, where he named his home Lipton House. In the following year it was ironic that, in spite of his attention to road safety, he was knocked down and injured after leaving his house, and it was some months before he recovered. His injuries possibly led to his retirement in 1935, at the age of seventy-two although he lived until 1943. He would have been interested to know that nos 26 and 27 Royal Terrace became the headquarters of the Lothian and Peebles Police in 1966. The two houses were severely damaged by fire in 1971.

Another long connection with Royal Terrace began with the arrival in 1925 of J Sloane Bayne,WS, who died in 1965. His daughter, Mrs Margaret Houston, continued to live there until her death in 1979. She was a Conservative town councillor.

## More Clergy

Two Moderators of the General Assembly of the Church of Scotland were the Very Rev.William Paterson, DD, LLD, FRSE and the Very Rev.Andrew Bogle, DD. Dr.Paterson came to no.5 in 1903 when he left the chair of Systematic Theology at Aberdeen University to take up the chair of Divinity in Edinburgh. He was chaplain-in-ordinary to the King in Scotland 1916-1939 and Moderator in 1919. While living in Royal Terrace he was an elder of Greenside church. Of his four sons and three daughters, two sons were killed in the war. After his wife's death in 1928 he moved to South Oswald Road. It was said that, with a twinge of endearing absent-mindedness, he could be intensely practical in the management of affairs.

Dr Bogle came to no.9 in 1916 on leaving North Leith United Free Church to become Secretary of the United Free Church, a post which he held until the Reunion of the Churches in 1929, when he became Secretary and Deputy at the Church of Scotland offices in George Street and left Royal Terrace. He became Moderator in the following year.

The Abbey Church in London Road, formed to serve part of Greenside parish and part of South Leith parish, acquired no.11 as its manse in 1910 and two ministers lived there. The first was the Rev. J R Sabiston who had been Minister of the Abbey Church since 1889. He knew each member of the Sunday School by name, which was quite a remarkable feat, as by 1899 it numbered over 900, with 84 teachers. He was a very big man and installed a huge bath which the next family found was so big that the water cooled before enough had run in.

The second minister was the Rev.Archibald Morrison who spent over twenty years in this manse from 1918. He was a Labour councillor for the city of Edinburgh from 1929 to 1931. His wife was a piano accompanist at their musical evenings. Every January the Morrisons hired trestle tables and gave tea to about fifty people who had made house-to-house collections for the church. They also entertained groups of African doctors including Dr Hastings Banda, later to be President of Malawi. This was because Mr

Morrison had heard that two Abyssinian doctors had been turned away from another Edinburgh church. Mrs Morrison was later given a book in gratitude, inscribed by Emperor Haile Selassie.

The manse then remained empty for most of the war years because of the cost of living in such a large house.

Another church serving this area was Lady Glenorchy's Free Church, opened in Greenside Place in 1846, a castellated building just south of the Playhouse. It was closed in 1978 (and became a paint warehouse) when the congregation merged with that of Barony and St James Place. The manse was in the tower of the church, but the Very Rev. James Harvey lived at 32 Royal Terrace from 1923, during the last few years of his long ministry there. He was known for his shrewd commonsense, mastery of detail and equitable temper, qualities which led to his appointment as Moderator of the Free Church in 1925. He was, additionally, Chaplain to the 7th Battalion, The Royal Scots, from 1911 until at least 1938. After leaving Lady Glenorchy's Church (and Royal Terrace) in 1929 he became Joint Senior Clerk of the General Assembly of the Church of Scotland.

## Doyen of the Consular Corps

A remarkable resident of Royal Terrace from 1901 was Professor Charles Sarolea who occupied two whole houses, 21 and 22, with his books, said to number a quarter of a million and to be the largest private library in Europe. He came to Edinburgh University in 1894 as the first lecturer and head of the French and Romance department. Two years later he was granted £5 by the university library committee towards the formation of a French class library. He was promoted to become the first Professor of French in 1918 and held that post until 1931.

Sarolea was Belgian by birth and he accompanied King Albert of Belgium as political adviser in 1920 on journeys to Brazil and West Africa. He was Belgian Consul from 1901 until his death in 1953 and in 1945 was elected Doyen of the Consular Corps in Edinburgh and Leith. During the two world wars he addressed many mass metings in America, Britain and on the Continent and raised over £100,000 for Belgian relief. He had a string of awards and honours from many countries.

Sarolea was a prolific writer, lecturer and editor on contemporary political topics. He was the author of at least twenty-five books and made Chinese and Japanese translations for anti-Bolshevist propaganda. His books were in every room of his two houses and double-banked up the stairs. He had many duplicates among his books, and he used to search by candlelight for any particular volume he wanted. He also collected furniture (including sixteen dining-tables for holding books), carpets, pictures, chandeliers, vast wall mirrors and other objects of art.

Part of Professor Sarolea's library at 22 Royal Terrace.

Charles Sarolea claimed a speaking knowledge of at least eighteen languages. He was twice widowed, his second wife dying in 1941. One of his nieces married John Bartholomew, whose grandfather had lived at 32 Royal Terrace.

## Distinguished Academics

Professor Robert Kerr Hannay and his wife Jane came to no.5 in 1925 and stayed there until her death in 1938. Prof. Hannay spent eight years (straddling the First War) as curator of the Historical Department in General Register House. From 1919 to his death in 1940, he was Fraser Professor of Scottish History and Palaeography becoming, additionally, Historiographer-Royal for Scotland in 1930.

Hannay was said to have a supersensitive dread of inaccuracy which led to a somewhat complicated style. Tall and handsome, he was a born raconteur, an excellent golfer and a musician of considerable gifts. In his earlier days he had played cricket for Stirlingshire and rugby football for Glasgow and Oxford universities.

Jane Hannay had been a mistress and house-mistress at St Leonard's School, St Andrews for ten years before their marriage in 1899. She was awarded an OBE in 1918 and a CBE in 1933, both for her social services. She had served as a member of the Scottish Savings Committee, of the

Central Committee on Training and Employment of Women (and vice-chairman of its Scottish committee) and of other bodies.

As an amateur musician, Professor Hannay would have known Sir Donald Tovey who lived at no.39 for ten years from 1930, having previously lived in George Square. Tovey was Reid Professor of Music from 1914 until his death in 1940. Born at Eton, where his father was an assistant master, Tovey embarked on musical composition from the age of eight. He never went to school, but from early childhood had been privately trained for the musical profession. He won a musical scholarship to Balliol College, Oxford. Soon after graduating in classics he gave a series of concerts of chamber music in London in 1900, followed by similar concerts in Berlin and Vienna, with the cooperation of Joachim and other artists. Joachim described him as the most learned musician in Europe.

Between 1906 and 1912 Tovey's concerts were organised by a committee under the title of Chelsea Concerts. In 1917, by means of the first series of concerts of the Reid Orchestra, he inaugurated a scheme whereby the professional orchestral players of Edinburgh and the university could more efficiently promote the interests of musical art.

Tovey was capable of playing at any moment any printed classical work on the piano, whether it were written for five or a hundred instruments, and whether he had ever heard it or not. He brilliantly set to music the poetry of Edward Lear, Lewis Carroll and Hilaire Belloc, along with advertisements and extracts from *Punch*. The music was never written down. He discussed interminably but when he digressed from his arguments (as he did at enormous length) it was found that the deviations were perfectly apposite and illuminating.

His reading, outside music, included detective stories, humorous works of all grades, especially verse, and the Encyclopaedia Britannica. At his home he entertained, and others were entertained by, visiting musicians such as Pablo Casals the cellist.

## Between the Wars

The sluggish market in Royal Terrace houses came to an end soon after the First War, when a number of new residents arrived. These included Dr A F Wilkie Millar who lived at no.7 from 1919 until his death in 1964. He was a greatly respected general practitioner, remembered for his courtesy and for visiting his patients by bicycle during the war years as a patriotic gesture to save fuel.

Thomas Anderson, at no.31 from 1927 for thirty-five years, was the first Director of the Seed Testing and Plant Registration Station at East Craigs, Corstorphine. He travelled to work by tram to the terminus at the Harp Hotel, where he transferred to a waiting taxi.

Royal Terrace facade.

A namesake of his, D A P Anderson, at no.38, a fancy stationer, was the father of the first Viscount Waverley who, as Sir John Anderson, was Permanent Under-Secretary of State at the Home Office 1922 to 1932 and then Governor of Bengal for five years. His letters home to his father in Royal Terrace told of the political unrest, terrorism, sickness and poverty, and of the social and economic reforms which he established. He twice narrowly escaped death as the result of attempts on his life.

On retiring from public service, Sir John was elected Member of Parliament for the Scottish Universities, which he represented as an independent member from 1938 until the abolition of university seats in 1950. The 'Anderson shelter' for protection from air raids was designed at his request. He held many government offices including Home Secretary and Chancellor of the Exchequer. He was one of the very few people to have held high office in the civil service as well as in the government. He was created a viscount in 1952 and OM in 1957 just before his death. His daughter, Mary Mackenzie, became Director of the Women's Royal Army Corps in 1967.

## Changing Use of Houses

During the 1920s a number of houses changed from family use to commercial residential establishments. Five houses became hotels, at least four became board residences, two nursing homes, two the premises of the Yorkshire United College (but one soon reverted to family use) and one a Church of Scotland hostel for many years. The trend continued in the 1930s, with a further four hotels, one board residence, two Scottish Residential Clubs and two more nursing homes. The Royal High School had a boarding house at 24 from 1927 until the school moved to Barnton in 1968.

Offices, also, began to take over some of the houses. The Scottish College of Accountants shared no.15 from 1920 with the Bible Students' Publishing Company. The Edinburgh Photographic Society, the Royal Scottish Society of Arts and the Edinburgh and District Radio Society all shared no.16 from 1920.

Immediately after the 1939-1945 War, when it must have been difficult for families to maintain big houses, there was a move to divide houses into flats. In 1945 the gardens committee decided not to oppose a petition to the Dean of Guild to convert no.12 into three flats. Two years later the committee considered the legal position regarding allocation of gardens assessments because of the continued division of houses, and recommended that proprietors creating flats should allocate the assessment and use of the gardens to one flat; other flat owners should be allowed to rent garden keys.

In recent years, several houses have been converted into flats and with more hotels and more offices, only four of the forty houses remain as family homes: one of them is also the Calton Gallery. Inevitably, some houses have deteriorated but no.4 has been lovingly restored and is now the home of the Scottish Chamber Orchestra and the Royal Danish Consulate.

# 5.
# CARLTON TERRACE

This inverted crescent joining Regent and Royal Terraces was named Carlton Place at first, becoming Carlton Terrace in 1842. Many of the houses are wedge-shaped, narrower at the back than the front. Each house has a small garden but the whole encloses Carlton Terrace Mews.

The plots were marked out in 1826, but no building was begun until later. John Neill, builder, was the first resident here. He came in 1830 with some of his ten children to no.17, one of the eight stances he had feued: four in Carlton Terrace and four in Royal Terrace. He was the only resident here for two years. He was then joined by seven more households, including a lamp and oil merchant (James Smith, from Salisbury Road) at no.8, Major John Barclay at no.7, the Misses Guthrie at 2 and Thomas Pender at 16. Neill died in 1837 and was buried in Old Calton Burying Ground.

## A New Church Building

Major Barclay had retired from the army and his sister Mary, younger by ten years, came with him. A few years after his death and ten years after the Disruption of 1843, she set up a trust of £10,000 for the erection of a Free Church of Scotland church in the New Town. She was anxious to assist in the growth of the new Free Church. She bequeathed income from the rest of her estate to be divided among ministers of the Free Church in Scotland and their sons, 'to assist in educating them for the ministry of the gospel in connection with the said Free Church' but no individual was to receive more than £10 per annum.

Three years later, in 1856, she replaced the requirement that the Church should be in the New Town with a directive that it should be 'in any portion of the town, new or old, or in the suburbs'. With a thought for the comfort of members of the congregation gathering at the entrance to the church, she

Rose Guthrie, a resident of Carlton Terrace.

stipulated that the doors were to be sheltered as far as possible from the winds. Six architects were invited to enter a competition for the design of the church.

Inevitably, Miss Barclay never saw the results of her beneficence because the money was not available until after her death. She died in 1858, the competition was held and the successful architect was Frederick Thomas Pilkington, whose church was built on the north west corner of Bruntsfield Links. Now called Barclay-Bruntsfield Church, it is still in use, by the Church of Scotland.

By a coincidence, the present owner of Miss Barclay's house, Hugh Cheape, is a kinsman of her neighbours and contemporaries, Miss Emily Guthrie and Miss Rose Guthrie of Craigie, Forfar at number 2. They were succeeded in that house by their niece the Hon. Mrs Jane (or Jean) Cheape, and the house was in the same family from 1832 to 1886. Although the Misses Guthrie never married they often had young relatives in their home, sometimes living there with a governess.

## Church Ministers

The Guthries' next-door neighbour for six years at no.3 was the Rev. Walter Tait. He was Minister of Trinity College Church from 1813 to 1833 and then moved from Ramsay Garden to 3 Carlton Place as the first occupant. In 1833 the Presbytery reported to the General Assembly that he 'had given countenance to certain extraordinary interruptions of public worship in his church on the Monday immediately after the communion, by a person [Thomas Carlyle] pretending to speak in the Spirit'. The General Assembly expressed their high disapprobation of these disorders and irregularities and remitted the case to the Presbytery. Tait was deposed in October 1833. He then became pastor of the congregation in Edinburgh of the Catholic Apostolic Church till his death in 1841.

In 1848, after Mr Tait's death, the mediaeval Trinity Church was sold to the North British Railway. The stones were numbered and laid aside on the Calton Hill for rebuilding on a new site. However, the Town Council caused many delays in the hope that the congregation would disappear and the church would not be needed. Meanwhile, many of the stones, which had been left in disarray, were taken for other purposes. In 1873 a new church was opened between High Street and Jeffrey Street, with over 800 on the roll. That building is now used as a brass-rubbing centre.

The Very Rev. Dr James Grant, Minister of St Mary's Parish Church, came to no.6 in 1854, in which year he became Moderator of the General Assembly of the Church of Scotland. He was also Secretary of the Scottish Bible Society for many years. He had earlier, in 1842, while Minister of South Leith, been suspended (with nine others) , for holding communion

Holyrood Palace from Regent Terrace photographed by Thomas Begbie, with the numbered stones from Trinity College Church visible in the foreground. (*The Cavaye Collection of Thomas Begbie prints, City Art Centre, Edinburgh*).

with the deposed ministers of Strathbogie. He had five sons and two daughters and his son Andrew became MP for Leith Burghs.

## A Restless Resident

Another of the first residents, Thomas Pender, was Comptroller and Accountant-General of Stamp Duties. He came from Salisbury Road and lived at no.16 for a year from 1833 before moving to 13 Royal Terrace for five years, then 16 Regent Terrace for two years and finally 1 Regent Terrace for one year. All of these houses were within a few minutes walk of his office in Waterloo Place. By 1841 he had five children and five resident servants.

## Commander of the Forces in Scotland

A distinguished army officer came to the terrace in 1833 from Whitehouse Villa, Bruntsfield Links. He was Lord Greenock and had come to Edinburgh in 1830 with the rank of Major-General. He had fought at the Battle of Waterloo, where he distinguished himself, having three horses shot under him. While serving with the British army of occupation he married Henrietta Mather in France in 1818 and repeated the marriage ceremony in England the following year.

While living here, Lord Greenock pursued his scientific interests and discovered a new mineral, sulphate of cadmium which was named greenockite after him. He was elected a Fellow of the Royal Society of Edinburgh.

Lord Greenock was appointed Commander of the Forces in Scotland and Governor of Edinburgh Castle in 1837. Six years later he succeeded his father, who had been a representative peer for Scotland and Ambassador to St Petersburg, as the second Earl of Cathcart. He then left the terrace to become Governor-General and Commander-in-chief in British North America (i.e. Canada). He finally retired as a full general.

His forbears had distinguished military careers. The first Baron Greenock was Warden of the West Marches in 1481. His heir and two other sons fell round the king at Flodden Field in 1513. The third baron fell at Pinkie in 1547; the 8th, 9th, 10th and 11th were all distinguished generals; and the famous General Cathcart who fell at Inkerman in 1854 was a son of the first earl and younger brother of the Carlton Terrace resident.

Lord Cathcart's house at no.12 was then occupied for nearly thirty years by James Cathcart, wine merchant of Leith, with his wife and six children and – in 1871 – seven resident servants.

## A Bogus Earl

Lord Greenock (as he still was) might have been perturbed or amused when the so-called Earl of Stirling rented Mr Neill's house at 17 in 1838.

As Alexander Humphreys he had an unusual early life. At the age of twenty, when he was living in France with his father, he was arrested by order of Napoleon on the resumption of hostilities in 1803. Although he remained a captive until 1814, he married in 1812 and his wife (appositely named Fortunata Bartoletti) introduced him to Mlle le Normand, a fortune-teller who predicted that he would attain distinction and opulence. He then learned of the dormant Earldom of Stirling and made enquiries about his descent.

Having adopted his mother's surname of Alexander in 1824, he went to the Palace of Holyrood in the following year to vote, as the Earl of Stirling, in the election of a representative peer. (The Act of Union of 1707 provided for Scottish Peers to elect, publicly, sixteen of their own number to sit in the House of Lords: the practice was discontinued by the Peerage Act of 1963). He voted at other peers' elections until his right was challenged. By then he had already created several baronets of Nova Scotia, to which land he said he was entitled. Alexander Humphreys visited the town of Stirling, where he was welcomed by the ringing of bells and was elected a burgess.

The self-styled earl was eventually committed to trial in 1839 on a charge of pretending to be the Earl of Stirling by means of seventeen forged documents. The trial was before four judges and lasted for five days; it was said that few cases in the criminal court had ever excited a greater interest, and that public opinion was in his favour. The three terraces must have been abuzz; of the eighteen landed men on the list of assize, five were neighbours – Captain David Brown of Park, George Cleghorn of Weens, John Hamilton Colt of Gartsherrie and Alexander McDuff of Bonhard all with houses in Regent Terrace, and John Greig of Lethangie, then living in Royal Terrace but earlier in Carlton Place and later in Regent Terrace. Two other neighbours were witnesses for the Crown, one being Isaac Bayley as agent for George Heriot's Hospital. The other was William Hume Lizars, who moved from Regent Terrace to Carlton Place in the year of the trial, and who gave evidence about the documents in the case, and especially the engraved map of Canada.

The jury found that the documents were forgeries but found it not proven that the claimant had either forged the documents himself or issued them knowing them to be forged. The forgeries were said to be quite clever and probably the work of Mlle le Normand, the fortune-teller. The false earl then left Edinburgh and disappeared into oblivion; he lived in America from 1846 until his death there in 1859.

## Large Households

At the time of the 1841 census Ann Hill, in her late twenties, was living with eleven teenage girls and two teenage servants at no.14. Apart from two pairs of sisters, they seem to have been unrelated. The householder there for thirty years from 1834 was Dr William Mackenzie of the Madras medical service. It is possible that he was in India in 1841, leaving his house to be used as a temporary boarding-house for daughters of other men serving overseas.

A widower, Dr Mackenzie had living with him in 1851 two sons, a married daughter with her three very young children, a sister-in-law (widow of a surgeon) and a friend, as well as five domestic servants. These last included a wet-nurse for the nine-month old baby and a male sick nurse, presumably for Dr Mackenzie. He cannot have been seriously ill, for he was still in his house in 1861 as well as his daughter with – now – five children and her husband, retired from the Bengal civil service and twenty years older than his wife. There were then four women servants with unspecified occupations.

The Rev.Charles Watson, DD, came to 13 Carlton Terrace in 1847 for ten years, having previously spent ten years in Royal Terrace. He had demitted office at Burntisland in 1837 because of a weakness in his voice. He joined the Free Church in 1843 but did not take up another appointment. He remained closely attached to the Free Church as an elder at St Andrew's, Edinburgh.

He had married Isabella Boog in 1821 and they had six sons and six daughters, of whom two sons and four daughters died in infancy. His eldest son, also Charles, declined nomination to the Moderatorship. One son became an eminent Edinburgh surgeon, Sir Patrick Watson, and another, Robert, was a noted conchologist and geologist and married Janet, daughter of Alexander Cowan of 35 Royal Terrace and niece of Duncan Cowan at 1 Carlton Terrace. A grandson, Charles B Boog Watson was a noted historian and antiquarian and for twenty-four years carried out invaluable voluntary research into the city records, working in an office provided for him in the City Chambers.

## Ships and Timber

The next occupant of no.14 was the founder of a firm of steamship owners, John Warrack. He came with his wife, three sons and a daughter and two daughters of his first marriage, along with a cook, laundry maid and housemaid. John Warrack earned a wide reputation in maritime affairs, contributing articles to the Encyclopaedia Britannica. He was elected by shipowners from both the east and west of Scotland to represent them on the Royal Commission on Loss of Life at Sea, 1884-1887. Apparently he managed to lighten the Commission's deliberations with his entertaining cross-examination of witnesses.

He found time to study many European languages and early German ecclesiastical music and was also president of the Speculative (debating) Society as well as a director of the National Bank of Scotland and of the Life Association of Scotland. He was sometimes mistaken for Garibaldi, the great Italian patriot and hero who raised 'The Thousand' – volunteers whose conquest of Sicily and Naples led to the unification of Italy. Warrack even gave sittings for busts of Garibaldi. By coincidence, the notice of Mr Warrack's death appeared on the centenary of Garibaldi's birth.

Three of his children who grew up in Carlton Terrace distinguished themselves in different ways. A daughter Grace was a considerable scholar who transcribed and edited *Revelations of Divine Love* written by Julian of Norwich in 1373: her work ran to nine editions. Among other books, she wrote one based on moving letters written by her half-brother – a second John Warrack – and his wife on the tragic death of a son at the age of four. Her great-nephew, Dr John Warrack, remembers visiting her and her sister, 'very proper old ladies with whom one was taken to tea on one's best behaviour'.

The second John, who grew up here, followed his father's footsteps in the steamship firm, but was also a scholar. He was the father of Guy Warrack, who became the first conductor of the BBC Scottish Orchestra in 1935. Another son of the first John Warrack managed to marry a nun in Italy.

As a ship owner, John Warrack may well have had business dealings with a timber merchant from Granton who came to no.7 on his marriage in 1876. This was Mitchell Thomson, who was Lord Provost of Edinburgh from 1897 to 1900 and was then created baronet, changing his surname to Mitchell-Thomson. He was largely responsible for Edinburgh Corporation's acquisition of the privately owned tramways and for organising the electric lighting of the city. He died suddenly in 1918 'having been seized with illness while attending a meeting of the directors of the Bank of Scotland'.

Sir Mitchell Mitchell-Thomson's only son William, who was born in Carlton Terrace and whose mother died as a result of his birth, was for some years engaged in West India business and also travelled extensively in Siberia, Manchuria and Korea. He was a Member of Parliament from 1906 to 1932 representing, successively, Lanarkshire North-West, Down, Glasgow Maryhill and South Croydon. He was Postmaster-General for five years and was created Baron Selsdon in 1932.

Mitchell-Thomson married for the second time in 1880 and it is possible that he met his second wife through his neighbours the Warracks, since her father was also a ship owner in Leith.

## Nineteenth Century Households

More than half of the householders at the 1841 census gave no details of their occupations except that they were independent, seven of them being women. The second most usual occupation was 'army' on either full or half pay.

The average household size from 1841 to 1891 ranged from seven to nine. Within that average there was considerable variation. At every census there was at least one house with fourteen residents. Many households had no children, but there were usually twenty-four children aged under fifteen in the terrace, as well as about half that number in their late teens. Carlton Terrace houses have no direct access to the big garden, so that small children would always have had to be taken there via the street.

Every household always included an average of three resident domestic servants. Apart from the usual occupations of cook, housemaid and table maid, in 1851 there were six lady's maids, two footmen and two butlers. Number 12, the home of a wine merchant, James Cathcart, had six servants in 1861 and seven in 1871, including a laundry maid, scullery maid, nurse and under nurse for four children aged three to twelve.

## The End of a Right to a Tied House

Edinburgh University provided an official residence in Old College for its librarian until 1881. It will be remembered that the Principal of the University, Dr Baird, at 13 Regent Terrace, had been indignant that the librarian, but not he, had an official residence.

John Small was appointed university librarian in 1854 at the early age of twenty-six. When his house in Old College was taken over to accommodate books he was awarded £70 in compensation and came to live at 10 Carlton Terrace with his mother and sister.

When Small became librarian, the University library was open to students only during the winter session, from 10 to 4. Students had to pay a deposit of £1 for every two books borrowed, which had to be returned within a fortnight. Professors were allowed to borrow twenty-five books and keep them for six weeks.

Mr Small was a conscientious worker. 'Such a thing as time for taking lunch was not in vogue. It was only on rare occasions that the indefatigable Mr Small went out for a few minutes.' He also took his turn at giving out books to students from the counter.In 1876 Mr Small reported that the library catalogue, being in manuscript, was not generally accessible to readers. Since funds were short, he instituted the practice of subscribing to an Edinburgh circulating library from which 150 volumes could be borrowed at any one time. Even in 1880 there was no lighting in the reading room in Old College, which made study very difficult on dark days.

Carlton Terrace.

After two years in Carlton Terrace Mr Small moved to 24 Regent Terrace where he died in 1886 after a long illness. His sister continued to live there until 1919.

## Nineteenth Century Residents

By 1851 there was a less marked preponderance of people of independent means or of army. Other occupations had started to arrive – two each of doctors, clergy and merchants (corn and wine) with one schoolmaster and one solicitor. The merchants gradually increased in number and in variety. Over the next forty years their trades included drugs, metals, commissions, timber and glass. Other occupations were a mixed collection of banker, brewer, ship-owner, Comptroller of Customs, company secretary, architect and artist.

During the nineteenth century five families moved house within the terrace, nine moved out to Regent or Royal Terrace, while seven moved in from those two terraces. Two families made a direct exchange of houses in 1905: W F Jackson, general manager of the North British Railway

Company, vacated 29 Royal Terrace in favour of William Gardner Sinclair, of the wholesale stationers Dobson, Molle and Co. in Easter Road, at 12 Carlton Terrace.

## Damage to Railings

Carlton Terrace might appear to be a quiet road which leads to nowhere in particular. Over the years there have been a number of accidents which resulted in serious damage to the railings of the front bank garden. Nowadays there is a recurring problem of cars driving into the railings. Previously the damage was caused by carts. In 1894 fifteen railings opposite no.8 were broken down, 'it is thought by a butcher's cart'.

A graphic account of a worse accident was given by a policeman and quoted in the garden committee minutes for 1903: At 7.30 am on Hogmanay,

> while James Dobbie, 23 years, son of and in the employment of Andrew Dobbie, Dairyman, 4 Antigua Street was driving a horse yoked to a milk-van along the street near 20 Regent Terrace, the horse took fright at a woman washing a doorstep and bolted, the horse coming against the iron railing at 27 Regent Terrace, breaking two of the iron tops of the railing and continuing its course into Carlton Terrace, where the horse came into contact with the railing at no.6 there, breaking 24 iron tops and cutting its windpipe causing it to fall where it was brought to a stand, and badly cut about the throat. The horse was removed to a stable in Regent Terrace Lane, where it immediately died.

The estimate for repairs was £4-5-0. However, the committee decided not to pursue Mr Dobbie for this sum, since he had been bankrupt a few years earlier and the committee members were sorry for him, having lost his horse. The occupier of no.6, who had such a rude awakening on Hogmanay, was George Mackie of J W Mackie and Sons Ltd of Princes Street, biscuit manufacturers to the Queen and the Prince of Wales.

## Marriages

Carlton Terrace obviously held attractions for newly married couples, who would be unlikely to be able to afford to live there nowadays. Ten years after Mitchell Thomson had brought his bride to Carlton Terrace, John Milligan, WS, did likewise. He had been born and brought up at 5 Royal Terrace and a younger brother inherited their father's house there. John Milligan was Session Clerk to Greenside Church; from 1899 he was the first Captain of the Boys' Brigade there, supervising five officers and forty boys. His son James (also WS) was born at no.10 and later married the girl next door, Amy Lorrain-Smith, whose father was Professor of Pathology.

Another newly married couple was James Peck and Winifred Knox, who came to no.11 on their marriage in 1911. He was then clerk to the Edinburgh School Board, one member (and later chairman) of which was his neighbour at no.5, Arthur Rose, a paint and varnish manufacturer, later created a baronet. After spending the four war years as an officer in the Royal Field Artillery, James Peck moved to London and started his civil service career. He later returned to Scotland, having entered the Scottish Education Department in 1927, where he became Permanent Secretary in 1936. While in that department he was invited to give the prizes at the Atholl Crescent School of Domestic Science, where he is reported to have told his audience, 'Some of you will be going on to teach and some to work in institutions but most of you will be entering the oldest profession'.

Sir James's wife Winifred was the sister of E V Knox ('Evoe' of *Punch*) and Monsignor Ronald Knox and of two other distinguished brothers. Winifred Peck was described by a university contemporary as a woman of distinguished grace and charm, with great brown eyes and overflowing sympathy. After graduating from Oxford she did welfare work with factory girls and district visiting. Later, she suffered greatly from the long illness and death in early manhood of the second of her three sons. She was the author of twenty-six books, mostly novels, but three were autobiographical accounts of her early life.

## *Distinguished Sculptors*

The two Rhind brothers, Birnie and Massey, were the first sculptors to live in any of the three terraces, apart from Henry Westmacott at 5 Royal Terrace in the 1830s. Both became RSAs.

Birnie Rhind came to live at no.3 in 1912 but had his studio at Eyre Terrace. He executed many public statues and memorials in Scotland and elsewhere. The nearest one to his home was the memorial on Edinburgh's North Bridge to men from the King's Own Scottish Borderers (The Edinburgh Regiment) who had died in Afghanistan, South Africa and on other battlefields. He was also responsible for the historical figures in canopied niches in the central doorway of the Scottish National Portrait Gallery.

Massey Rhind, the younger brother, retired in 1930 and took over his brother's house, having spent most of his professional life in the USA. He executed a great deal of work in almost every state there, including a large bronze equestrian memorial of George Washington and heroic statues of four later presidents. He was responsible for a statue of Robert Burns in Pittsburg and for all the bronze decorations on the Carnegie Institute there and also for many others in Canada.

## Change of Use of Houses

The character of the terrace began to change. The first private hotels came to Carlton Terrace in the late 1920s at 11, 14, 15 and 16. The Office for the Commissioner for Special Areas was at 13 and 14 in the mid-1930s, the Commissioner being Sir Arthur Rose who had earlier lived at no.5. Those office premises were successively used by the Royal Observer Corps and the Scottish Home Department, whose head, Sir Norman Duke, lived at 30 Regent Terrace from 1947 until his death in 1969.

Mr W T Henry bought no.13 in 1934 and applied for variation of the conditions in his title deeds, so that he could convert the house into two or more dwellings. The application was strongly opposed by a large number of residents in the three terraces and by the superiors (George Heriot Trust). The case was heard by Sheriff C H Brown, KC, who refused the application, finding that no dwelling-house in Carlton Terrace or in either of its neighbours Royal and Regent Terraces, had been converted into separate dwellings, nor had any application been made to convert any house in these three terraces. Mr Henry, the sheriff said, had failed to prove that he could not let the house as a single dwelllng.

After the sheriff's finding, Mrs Moller of no.5 wrote to her daughter Asta, 'As you can imagine, there is great excitement in the Terraces. Sheriff Brown gave the Terraces a very nice puff and I hope it will do good'.

In the same year, Mrs Moller also wrote to her daughter, 'Mrs Barker had a bridge party last night for twenty ladies and they had a savoury supper of six different kinds and cakes from Atholl Crescent [school of domestic science]. A savoury supper is the correct thing now!' Mrs Barker lived next door at no.4 and her husband was a medical practitioner who was also the President of the Scottish Psychical Society.

Mrs Moller and her husband, a Danish export and import merchant, had come to live in no. 5 in 1923 after three years in 20 Regent Terrace. Mrs Moller was one of the first two women to be elected a member of the gardens committee in 1925. Her two unmarried daughters lived in the house until their deaths. One of them, Dr Asta Moller, was a lecturer in economics at Edinburgh University and was a fount of knowledge about the history of the three terraces. Unfortunately the results of her researches could not be found when she died in 1985 aged ninety-four. Although the Mollers rented their house in Regent Terrace for such a short time, they left behind a tangible reminder of their stay. When the hall linoleum was lifted about forty years later, some old Danish newspapers were found underneath. Asta Moller was delighted to be given them, especially as one described the visit to Edinburgh of the Danish Prince Charles in 1896. Prince Charles that year married Maud, the daughter of the future King Edward VII and Queen Alexandra (herself a Danish princess) and in 1905 he was offered and accepted the crown of the new kingdom of Norway, becoming King Haakon VII.

Shortly before the Earl of Cassilis succeeded his father as Marquess of Ailsa in 1938 he acquired no.6 as his town house. After his death in 1943, his widow the Dowager Marchioness and her two sisters lived here, one being the Dowager Duchess of Grafton and the other Miss Blanche MacTaggart-Stewart. Their house had a huge water-butt in the front area to catch rain water, used for washing clothes. There were also lavatories for servants in a cellar under the pavement, whereas other houses had them in a back area.

## A Flamboyant Figure

Sir Iain Moncreiffe of that Ilk lived at no.1 for a few years until 1953. He was then Unicorn Pursuivant of Arms and later Albany Herald. He was eccentric, erudite and entertaining, the self-styled Master Snob. Tremendously knowledgeable about genealogy, which he described as fun, he traced my own family – for fun – back to Queen Margaret of Scotland and King John of Jerusalem and beyond.

Sir Iain's wife was the Countess of Erroll in her own right, as chief of the Hay Clan. As hereditary Lord High Constable of Scotland, she was the senior Great Officer of the Royal Household in Scotland.

## Present Use of Houses

The private hotels have gradually reverted to residential housing and today there is only one hotel in the terrace, spread over three houses. The only other non-residential premises are those of the Lothian Health Board, also occupying three houses.

# 6.

# REGENT, ROYAL AND CARLTON TERRACE MEWS

Playfair's plan of 1819 for Regent, Royal and Carlton Terraces showed a short double row of mews at the backs of Regent and Royal Terraces, projecting into the pleasure ground. Also, immediately opposite those mews he indicated an isosceles triangle layout of mews to be enclosed by the gardens of Carlton Place (later, Terrace) and with an opening into a dog-leg lane dividing Carlton Place from the other two terraces. The first of these rows of mews was eventually built to that plan, but Carlton Terrace Mews changed its shape in order to open further north into the lane.

The mews were slow to be built and were not completed until the end of the nineteenth century. At ground level they housed horses and carriages: their upper floors provided living quarters for coachmen, usually with an outside stair, only one of which remains.

At the 1841 census two families lived in Regent Terrace Stable Lane at its east end, both householders being described as male servant. John Davidson had a wife and four small children; Robert Mackenzie had a wife and three small children and three lodgers. By 1851 four families lived in what was then called Regent Meuse Lane. Three were headed by coach proprietors or coach hirers who each had up to three employees living with them. The fourth was Alexander Diey, a coachman with five children, including two blacksmith sons and a dressmaker daughter. Two other unmarried coachmen each lived alone in other mews properties.

Ten years later again, in 1861, Regent Terrace Lane housed eleven families. Again, most were coach hirers or coachmen. One householder was a butler whose wife and daughter (both called Isabella Comb) were listed here while he was included in the residents of 36 Royal Terrace. There were twenty-eight children aged under fifteen but practically no adult children. In addition, one coachman and his family lived in Carlton Terrace Lane.

One of the coach hirers, Alexander Mann, had his home here (at what later became 20 Royal Terrace Mews) for over thirty years. One of his sons became an insurance clerk and the other a cab clerk, having his own home at 5 Regent Terrace Meuse in 1881. A complaint was made at the gardens AGM of 1882, about 'the practice of the proprietor of one of the stables and houses over same who occupies it himself (Mann, cab hirer) of having clothes constantly hanging out at his windows drying, and also of throwing rubbish into the gardens.'

Several of the houses in Regent and Royal Terrace Mews still have a gadget for hanging out washing from the upper windows on a line which goes over pulleys at either side of the mews. The alternative was to hang wet washing from pulleys on the ceiling. Clothes could be washed in a boiler served by a brick fireplace at the far end of the mews. Coachmen were not allowed to wash their coaches outside, but had to do the job in their coach-houses.

The number of inhabited mews houses in Regent Terrace Lane dropped to seven in 1871, but those in Carlton Terrace Lane (later Mews) increased to seven. There were then twenty-six children under fifteen in all the mews houses. These children were not allowed to play in the big gardens which belonged to the proprietors of the three terraces. Houses in Carlton Terrace Lane now had numbers, from 1 to 17 (not all inhabited). Buildings in that mews were not allowed windows overlooking Carlton Terrace houses and gardens.

From 1871, adult children of these householders had a variety of occupa-

Carlton Terrace Mews.

A local coachman's account, 1893

tions. Sons were clerks, a ropespinner, a plumber and joineryman and a pupil-teacher. Daughters were dressmakers, a confectioner and a milliner.

Regent Terrace Lane had been redesignated as Regent Terrace Meuse on the south side and Royal Terrace Meuse on the north by 1881, with ten houses inhabited and nine uninhabited. There were more coachmen than coach proprietors. All the houses were numbered in one sequence by 1881, starting at the east end of Regent Terrace Meuse, continuing back along Royal Terrace Meuse and then all round Carlton Terrace Lane, in which only eight out of fourteen houses were inhabited. Householders were still predominantly coachmen.

The situation was much the same in 1891. In 1893, I and R Leggat, coach hirer of Regent Terrace Lane (possibly the dog-leg lane?) was advertising first class broughams with superior horses and 'a large brake for Pic-Nics'. In 1905 Mr Leggatt was described as a merchant.

There were half as many properties in the mews as in the terraces, showing that not all residents of terrace houses could keep their own carriages or horses there. During the nineteenth century the presence of coach hirers living in the mews suggests that for many terrace residents it was more convenient to hire a carriage (the equivalent of telephoning for a taxi today) than to own one.

Horses continued to be stabled in the mews, including Baroness Burton's polo ponies in Carlton Terrace Lane early in the twentieth century.

Shortly before the 1914-18 War coachmen began to be replaced by chauffeurs, working for residents of the three terraces. The cars they drove included Daimlers, Lanchesters, a Crossley, a Rolls, a Packard and Mr Bertram's maroon Buick with white-walled tyres. The loose-boxes, coach houses and harness rooms became garages or workshops. Some still retain their original fittings.

Haylofts and some garages have since been changed into living accommodation, but most houses still have garages attached. Practically all of the houses used to be tied houses. From the 1930s, when fewer people had chauffeurs, their former employers usually gave them the opportunity to rent their homes, and some were able to buy them.

Houses in the mews were originally very simple, with one cold water tap which was often in the stable (or garage). Water was heated in a big iron kettle on a gas ring. Up to the 1930s some still had gas lighting. Clothes were then taken on a small hand-cart to be washed at the 'steamie' or wash-house near the top of Abbeymount.

A colourful resident of 24 Carlton Terrace Mews from 1928 to his death in 1976 was David W Hyslop. As a conscientious objector in the 1914-18 War he looked after horses at Aldershot. He was then a sports reporter for the *Scotsman* and a courier for Mackay Bros, travel agents, but in 1924 became a second-hand bookseller with premises in an upstairs salon at 111a George Street and later in College Street. He was the first man in Britain to import Odeon and Polydor gramophone records. He had eight stores for his books, mostly in old houses, and he sold many books at auction in New York. His personal collection of 100,000 books he kept in his five-car garage and in his flat above, causing the ceiling beam to drop ten inches in the centre. He was an avid reader with a phenomenal memory, and a keen hill walker.

Nowadays, mews properties are modernised and are sought after as homes. Those in Carlton Terrace Mews enjoy an attractive shared garden in the middle, which was the site for an Anderson air-raid shelter in the 1939-45 War and also for a Coronation street party for all mews residents in 1953, although the residents of the two sets of mews have usually comprised two separate communities.

# 7.

# CALTON HILL PLEASURE GROUND

An integral part of Playfair's plan was the construction of a 'pleasure ground' on the land enclosed by Regent and Royal Terraces, by a wall at the east side of Calton Hill and by the stable lane which later became mews properties. The garden extended to more than eleven acres and the ninety-three stance-holders were – and still are – statutorily responsible for the maintenance of this landscaped garden, through the payment of an annual assessment. Playfair expected this feature to attract residents from the New Town or the West End of Edinburgh. The gardens were originally called the Calton Hill Pleasure Ground, but are now known as the Regent, Royal and Carlton Terrace Gardens.

In 1830 a committee was appointed for carrying the plan of the pleasure ground into execution, for laying and planting as well as letting part of the garden for nursery ground. Professor Robert Graham and Dr Patrick Neill both gave professional advice. There seems to have been no truth in the belief that the gardens were laid out by Joseph Paxton.

Robert Graham was Regius Professor of Botany and Keeper of the Edinburgh Royal Botanic Garden. Patrick Neill, LLD was a printer by trade and also a skilled gardener. He was a pteridologist, botanist and horticulturalist and was secretary of the Wernerian Natural History Society. He wrote an article on gardening for the Encyclopaedia Britannica, and he had helped to create East Princes Street Gardens and given advice on treeplanting in George Square. Dr Neill drew up detailed planting lists, and the plants were supplied by a local nurseryman, Alexander Wright of Greenside Place.

There are no recorded details of the layout of the gardens, except that in 1832 the committee authorised completion of the work on a well, including a pump. This pump was still working a hundred years later. In 1843 a bridge was built connecting two high banks at the west end of the gardens.

## Feu Charter

A contract of feu was entered into between the Governors of George Heriot's Hospital and the feuars of stances in Regent Terrace, Carlton Place and Royal Terrace on 20 April 1829. Ground of over eleven acres was thereby feued as 'ornamental pleasure ground' and an annual assessment payable by each stance-holder 'should not exceed ten pounds per annum'. For over a hundred years, until 1966, this limit was acceptable but thereafter the assessments provided insufficient funds for the maintenance of the gardens. A private Act of Parliament was passed in 1970 to remove the limit of £10. The 1829 contract of feu reserved the right of the superiors (the Governors of George Heriot's Hospital) to resume up to one acre for the erection of a public building 'which is not to be of an offensive nature'. Fortunately this right was never claimed.

An assessment of three shillings per foot of frontage was to be paid by proprietors from 1830. Originally assessments were collected by the gardener, who was therefore often absent from the garden. The committee agreed, in 1835, either to employ someone else or to pay the gardener for extra hours.

Proprietors were also, from time to time, charged for capital outlay such as repairs to the street.

A perennial problem, first mentioned in the minutes for 1834, was that of the 'improper use of keys for the doors of the pleasure ground'. In 1876 the committee authorised the issue of new keys to the gardens, in order 'to exclude numerous persons not residing in the Terraces who have got possession of keys'.

Membership of the committee from 1834 comprised three residents from each of the three terraces, in addition to the chairman and a representative of George Heriot's Hospital. One member from each terrace retired each year by rotation. This requirement later lapsed but since 1964 committee members have served for a maximum of six years.

Also in 1834, a request was made to the Lord Provost and magistrates to fence in the ground at the east end of the High School, to prevent the boys from getting into the gardens.

## Gardeners

In December 1831 the first gardener, Edwin Neilson, was engaged at a wage of ten shillings per week. He was also responsible for collecting assessments from proprietors, and additionally he and subsequent gardeners had certain policing responsibilities. In 1834 he was ordered to endeavour to discover who had carried off the forty or fifty 'pailing stabs' from the grounds. He was also expected to watch the gardens after his working hours and on Sundays, but it is not clear whether he was paid for these extra hours.

Nearly a century later, in 1925, the gardener was employed to patrol the gardens from 8 to 10 pm during July and August and to challenge anyone whom he considered to be an unauthorised user of the gardens. He reported seventy-three such persons, most of them from houses in Royal Terrace, perhaps boarders or lodgers. Policing by the gardener continued until 1939. Possibly because of these extra duties, the gardener was forbidden (in 1924) to accept employment from any proprietors outside his working hours. This probibition was repeated in 1936, but in 1942 the ban was lifted. Two assistant gardeners were usually employed during the summers.

## Regulations

Regulations for the use of the gardens were first drawn up in 1832. The committee resolved to prevent by every possible means the using of fire-arms and the playing of quoits except upon the ground appointed for the latter purpose. During that year a complaint was made about the son of Mr Adie, civil engineer, of 10 Regent Terrace for persisting in choosing his own ground for playing quoits to the danger of children. At that time Princes Street Gardens were also private but had more restrictions on their use: smoking was forbidden, as were bath-chairs, dogs, pigs and little boys.

## Children

There were once a great many children under fifteen in the three terraces, ranging from a peak of 163 in 1841 (although fourteen houses were not yet built) to only eighty-six in 1891, compared with about thirty in 1992. The eleven acre garden must have been well used by all those children, some of them accompanied by nursemaids.

Not all of the children using the gardens were well-behaved. As early as 1835, the gardens minutes recorded that a notice had been sent to all houses that any young people found injuring plants or shrubs, or playing games which injure the grass, would be sent to the police. Notice-boards to that effect were then said to have been removed by six boys, all named. The gardener was instructed to take letters to their parents. The father of three of them threatened prosecution of the committee for alleged defamation of the character of his sons, evidence against whom had been from one boy only. A reward of one guinea was paid to the labourer who had given evidence against that boy who, in turn paid £3 damages. However, the committee then repaid half of this fine, because he had been 'only one of the parties concerned in the outrage'.

In November 1897, seventeen sons of proprietors wrote to the treasurer 'asking that an anonymous charge of card-playing be investigated'.

Dr Patrick Neill, who helped to design the gardens. (*Modern Athenians*).

## Entertainment and Sport

The committee unanimously agreed in 1838 and in 1839 to a request from the Commanding Officer of the 7th Dragoon Guards for their band to play once a week in the gardens. The concert was to be on Thursdays, from 2 to 5 pm, for inhabitants and their friends. Thanks were later sent to Lord Greenock (later the Earl of Cathcart) who was the Commander of the Forces in Scotland and lived first at 5 and then at 12 Carlton Terrace, and to the commanding officers of the regiments whose bands of music had performed during the summer.

In 1883 two tennis courts were formed at the foot of the slope from the

The Duc de Bordeaux,
grandson of Charles X of France, in Calton Hill Pleasure Ground.

Tennis party in the gardens:
Mrs William Bertram with her brother and sister and friends, 1887.

high wall, at a cost of about £12 each, but it was noted that they had 'not been played on except twice or thrice'. A tennis tournament was held during the last week of June in 1887. But in 1889 the two courts were returned to their original state, presumably lawn. Instead, a brick dust court had been laid close to the brick tool-house, which had been built in 1885 with a privy behind it.

After suggestions that players should provide their own net, rather than one supplied by the gardens, in 1912 Mrs Gardner Sinclair, 29 Royal Terrace, presented a first class tennis net. She also gave sheet-iron to cover the railway sleepers at the end of the extension of the tennis court to the south. In the following year her husband (and by now they had moved to 35 Royal Terrace) offered to present two shelters to the gardens. The committee recommended one on the centre of the top bank and one at the east side of the tennis court. It is not clear whether both were built, but the latter was known as the Sinclair shelter: it was destroyed by fire in 1979.

The Rev. Mr Thornton (26 Regent Terrace), whose family owned Thornton's toy and sports shop in Princes Street, presented a new net for the tennis court in 1931. Bicycles and tricycles were banned from the gardens from 1885. By 1894 there were annual sports in the gardens. There is no record of the formation of the pitch and putt golf course, but in 1894 a proposal was made to substitute holes in the golfing ground for posts: the task was completed the following year, with pins and flags. Games may have been forbidden on Sundays. Tennis and golf were certainly banned on Sundays after the 1914-18 War.

Fireworks in the gardens on the Queen's Birthday were 'an old institution' when, in May 1898, Miss Anderson of 8 Regent Terrace complained that a rocket had pierced a pane of glass in a high back bedroom of her house.

The first mention of snow-sports is in February 1900, with complaints that the daughter of Sheriff Brand, 13 Royal Terrace, the son of Mrs Inglis, 12 Royal Terrace, and the daughters of Mr Currie, 4 Royal Terrace had 'again persisted in tobogganing to the injury of the ground'.

The annual meeting in 1924 rejected the motion of Mr Moller of 5 Carlton Terrace that proprietors 'be allowed to attach aerial wires to a tree in the gardens provided the same is in close proximity to his private grounds'.

Summer garden parties for residents have been held intermittently over the years. These were usually purely social events, but were at times also used to raise funds for the maintenance of the gardens.

The gardens in snow, 1991. (*James D Farrar*).

## Garden Rubbish

The gardener found difficulty, in 1882, in consuming or disposing of the quantity of garden clearings and rubbish laid down in the garden by nurserymen employed to work in the private back greens of terrace houses. He was empowered to get the accumulations carted away at the general expense. Until then, carts had been able to enter the gardens directly from the stable lane (or mews) but in 1892 it was reported that the George Heriot Trust would shortly stake off and enclose the area of ten unbuilt stances and the lane between them at the west end of Regent Terrace Lane. A cart entrance was made (presumably the present double gates) in 1895.

## Railway Tunnels

Some consternation was caused by three Railway Bills in 1891. The Caledonian Railway, Edinburgh and Leith line, proposed a tunnel under the main gardens and those of 30 and 31 Royal Terrace. The Edinburgh and Leith Junction line proposed a tunnel under the gardens and under 10, 11 and 12 Carlton Terrace. The North British Railway (Waverley) Station line proposed a tunnel seventy feet down under a corner of the gardens near the High School and 1-4 Regent Terrace. Fortunately, all three bills were withdrawn.

## Outside Requests for Use of Gardens

From time to time the committee has considered requests from outside bodies to use the gardens. For instance, in 1892 it turned down a request from Mr Bruce, 10 Regent Terrace, and Mr Bartholomew, 32 Royal Terrace, for members of the British Association to be invited to a garden party in August. The reason given was that 'all or nearly all of the proprietors will probably be from home'.

Four years later Mrs Turcan, 33 Royal Terrace, was given permission to hold a 'small cake and apron sale' in the gardens.

A request from two other residents, Mrs Liebenthal, 34 Regent Terrace and Mrs Blair, 9 Regent Terrace, was refused in 1900. As joint secretaries of the Calton Circle of the Scottish Children's League of Pity they had wanted to stage a pastoral play in the gardens.

Not surprisingly, the committee refused a request in 1951 from the Oxford University Dramatic Society (via Lord Primrose) to stage performances in the gardens for two weeks, with an expected audience of 700 people nightly. There was no offer of payment, but merely for any damage to be made good.

During the Second World War the gardens were lent for military purposes. The St Andrew's House Company Home Guard was given permission, in 1941, to use the gardens on Sundays from 10.30 to 12.30 for organised classes in musketry and bombing ('dummy bombs only'). Three years later women of the Auxiliary Territorial Service, based in Royal Terrace, were given permission to drill in the gardens daily from 7.45 to 8.15am. Soldiers resident in the terraces were allowed to use the gardens free from 1942. Experimental trenches had been dug in the gardens in 1938 as air raid protection.

## Damage to Front Bank Garden

In 1894 a man in the employment of Brown, a chimney sweep of Norton Place, was fined one shilling for depositing soot in the Front Bank. A week later he repeated the offence and was fined five shillings or two days. On his third offence he was fined seven shillings and sixpence.

More serious was – and still is – damage to the railings between the Front Bank garden and Regent and Carlton Terraces. In 1886 twelve railings opposite 10 Regent Terrace were broken by the cart of Anderson, fish-monger, 'who is to pay'.

## Royal High School

As next door neighbour, it was inevitable that the Royal High School should look to the possibility of expanding into the gardens. The first approach to the committee was in 1943, when the Town Clerk inquired about the possibility of acquiring the gardens for the school. The request was refused because it was outwith the terms of the feu charter.

The next approach was not made until 1957, when the City Treasurer indicated that he might seek some ground in the south west corner of the gardens for an extension of the Royal High School. The following year a meeting was held in the school between the gardens committee, city officials, the rector of the school, members of the education committee and others. The proposal was for a four-acre site to be used for classrooms, workshops, a gymnasium and a swimming pool. The houses at 1, 2 and 4 Regent Terrace would no longer be needed for class-rooms and would be restored to domestic use. Again, there was opposition from residents and the education committee finally decided to move the school to Barnton.

## Royal Visits

Members of the public were admitted to the front bank garden in 1886 to view Queen Victoria's procession from Holyrood to the International Exhibition. Six watchmen were hired from the chief constable on that day.

At the beginning of the twentieth century tickets were allocated annually to proprietors to watch the King and Queen and also the High Commissioner to the General Assembly of the Church of Scotland process along Regent Road.

## Royal Terrace Gardens

The Royal Terrace Gardens, in the space between Royal Terrace and London Road, were laid out in 1831 in consultation with William Playfair, including a footpath especially requested by Charles X, then in exile at the Palace of Holyroodhouse. The George Heriot Trust decided to let out the ground for nursery or garden purposes and – in 1836 – built a small cottage for a gardener at the western end of the gardens. The cottage was designed by Playfair and was called Royal Terrace Gardens House and is still inhabited.

The first tenant of this cottage was John Niven, who proved to be an unsatisfactory tenant, allowing his horse to be pastured in the gardens, failing to lock the gates at night and allowing children to run wild.

The next tenant, James Turner, was more successful and stayed from 1841 to 1859. He was followed by George Wood, who was in the cottage until 1871 but he, also, was asked to leave because he was allowing families from Windsor Street, Leopold Place and Blenheim Place to dry and bleach their clothes in one part of the garden.

George Wood, who had six children, described himself in the 1861 and 1871 censuses as a florist, as was his thirteen-year-old son; an older son was a hairdresser and a daughter a confectioner. The cottage also housed a second family – two dressmakers in 1861 and a ship broker's clerk with his wife in 1871. By 1891, the second householder was the gardener's father with his daughter.

Meanwhile, the proprietors of Royal Terrace houses contributed to the cost of a parapet and railing along the top of the gardens, but their petition for a bowling green was refused.

The existing railings must have proved unsatisfactory, for in 1891 the town council asked the trust to erect a cope and railing along the whole length of the gardens. The town council then took a 25-year lease of the gardens, at £25 p.a., on condition that a park-keeper should reside in the cottage, the grounds being used solely as ornamental pleasure gardens, and the gates along Royal and Carlton Terraces were to be restricted to keyholders in those two terraces.

The railings were removed during the Second World War, when many railings were needed for melting down to assist in the manufacture of aircraft. The public lavatories in the north-east corner of the gardens were built in 1955.

Professor Sarolea in the gardens.

# EPILOGUE

The area covered by this book is unique in being close to the centre of a capital city with splendid views of the Palace of Holyroodhouse and Arthur's Seat to the south and of the Firth of Forth to the north, as well as having large open spaces, both public and private.

The buildings have mostly been well preserved or restored. In more than one and a half centuries since the Playfair plan was conceived, there have been remarkably few major changes in the buildings apart from the demolition of the prison and the subsequent building of St Andrew's House.

Some alterations to the character of the area have been seen over the years, such as the change of use of a number of houses into hotels or offices and the division of others into flats, but it is still mainly residential, as Playfair intended.

If pressures for a Scottish Parliament were to succeed and the old Royal High School were to be used for such a purpose, one can only speculate what effect this would have on the neighbouring area.

# PRINCIPAL SOURCES

Birrell, J F, *An Edinburgh Alphabet*, 1980
Books of the Old Edinburgh Club
Byrom, Constance, *The Pleasure Gardens of Edinburgh New Town*, unpubl. PhD thesis 1984
Calton Hill Pleasure Ground committee minutes, from 1825
Census returns of 1841, 1851, 1861, 1871, 1881, 1891
Cockburn, Lord, *A Letter to the Lord Provost on the Best Ways of Spoiling the Beauty of Edinburgh*, 1849
Crombie, B W, *Modern Athenians*, 1857
Dictionary of National Biography
Edinburgh Room, Central Library: press cuttings
Fasti ecclesiae scoticanae, 1915-61
Gifford, John, Colin McWilliam and David Walker, *The Buildings of Scotland: Edinburgh*, 1984
Grant, James, *Old and New Edinburgh*, 1882
Post Office street directories
Ross, William, *The Royal High School*, 2nd edition, 1949
Smith, Charles J, *Historic South Edinburgh*, vols. 3 and 4, 1986 and 1988
Steuart, Archibald Francis, *The Exiled Bourbons in Scotland*, 1908
Swinton, A (ed), *Report of the Trial of Alexander Humphreys or Alexander Claiming the Title of the Earl of Stirling*, 1839
Taverner, Neil, *The Church on the Hill*, c.1989
Watson, Charles B B, *Alexander Cowan of Moray House and Valleyfield*, 1915-17
Whitson, Thomas B, *Lord Provosts of Edinburgh*, 1932
Youngson, A J, *The Making of Classical Edinburgh*, 1986
Personal communications

# PICTURE CREDITS

# INDEX